LUCKY
FOR ME

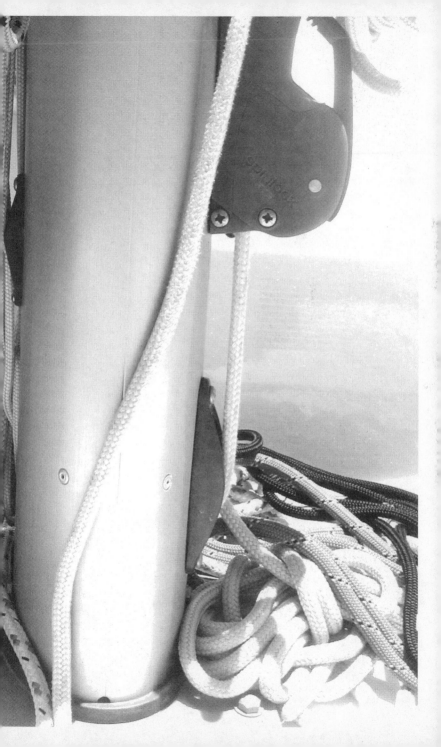

LUCKY
FOR ME

FRANK ROBSON

HarperCollins*Publishers*

Quotes from *Dogs Never Lie About Love* by Jeffrey Masson, published by
Jonathan Cape. Reprinted by permission of The Random House Group Ltd.

HarperCollins*Publishers*

First published in Australia in 2007
by HarperCollins*Publishers* Australia Pty Limited
ABN 36 009 913 517
www.harpercollins.com.au

HarperCollins*Publishers*
25 Ryde Road, Pymble, Sydney, NSW 2073, Australia
31 View Road, Glenfield, Auckland 10, New Zealand
1–A, Hamilton House, Connaught Place, New Delhi – 110 001, India
77–85 Fulham Palace Road, London, W6 8JB, United Kingdom
2 Bloor Street East, 20th floor, Toronto, Ontario M4W 1A8, Canada
10 East 53rd Street, New York NY 10022, USA

National Library of Australia Cataloguing-in-Publication data:

Robson, Frank.
   Lucky for me.
   ISBN 978 0 7322 8505 0 (pbk.).
   1. Robson, Frank. 2. Terriers – Queensland – Biography.
   3. Dogs – Queensland – Biography. 4. Human–animal relationships
   – Queensland. I. Title.
636.7550929

Cover design by Matt Stanton
Internal design by Natalie Winter
Photographs on pages xii, 30, 40, 126, 160, 194 and 223 by David Sproule
Photograph on page 140 by Graeme Parkes
Typeset in 10.5/16.5 Sabon by Helen Beard, ECJ Australia Pty Limited
Printed and bound in Australia by Griffin Press
79gsm Bulky Paperback used by HarperCollins*Publishers* is a natural,
recyclable product made from wood grown in a combination of sustainable
plantation and regrowth forests. It also contains up to a 20% portion of
recycled fibre. The manufacturing processes conform to the environmental
regulations in Tasmania, the place of manufacture.

8 7 6 5 4   08 09 10 11

To Mim's mum,
for helping us get Lucky

Sea dog: an experienced or old sailor.

Seadog: another word for fogbow or fogdog.

Fogdog: a whitish spot sometimes seen in fog near the horizon.

— Collins English Dictionary

PROLOGUE

Late at night, a small dog races north towards the Great Barrier Reef on board an old wooden sailboat. It's a rough passage — his first on the open sea — yet Lucky isn't afraid. He sits calmly on the sofa in the main cabin, his circular brown eyes following my movements at the wheel. I'm less calm, but trying not to show it. We're 40 nautical miles off the coast of Queensland threading a course among coral reefs; the wind is gusting over 30 knots, and the night is so dark it feels as though the boat is falling endlessly into black space.

Then a boisterous cross-sea develops, breaking over the decks and buffeting us from side to side. Wrestling with the wheel, I spot Lucky being catapulted from the sofa to the cabin floor. He's up in an instant, stumpy legs powering him back onto the seat. When our eyes meet, he tilts his head and gives one of his famous snorts: 'Kwok!' (Meaning: 'Go easy!')

He's bounced from his perch several more times before I notice him tugging at one of the sofa cushions. He nudges it here and there, falls, drags himself up again, persisting until he's positioned the cushion so that he can wedge himself between it and the back of the sofa. Then he rolls onto his back, gives a couple of 'Kaarks!' (meaning: 'Yeesss!'), and goes to sleep.

I already know Lucky is no ordinary little mutt. Yet I can't quite accept what I've seen, and glance over at Des, the friend sailing with me. 'Jesus,' he says, shaking his head. 'What sort of dog *is* that?'

As we watch Lucky snoring upside-down on his reorganised sofa, I'm distracted (not for the first time) by a sense that he may not be a dog at all, but some kind of explorer from an alternative life pool who likes to hang out with humans. We race on towards Lady Musgrave

Island, a coral atoll and reef-fringed lagoon offshore from Gladstone, at the southern tip of Queensland's Great Barrier Reef.

The next time I glance at the sofa, Lucky isn't on it. My eyes go straight to the sliding door leading to the deck — the door I'd solemnly promised my absent partner, Leisa, would *always* be kept shut at sea. It's half-open. Weak with dread, I stumble out onto the plunging deck. No Lucky. Clinging to the safety rails, I inch around the cabin structure. Wind howls among the stays; cold water rushes over my ankles. Then I see him. He's drenched, and so tiny against the immense, buffeting blackness I can't believe he's still on his feet. He stands, wobbling, right at the edge of the deck.

I almost shout his name, then remember how he sometimes regards being called as the signal for a game of chasey. So I get down and crawl towards his blind side. I realise he's piddling in the same instant that I grab him around the ribs with such force he yelps and tries to bite me. But I hang on, laughing and screaming over the wind to my anxious mate at the wheel, 'I got him, Des! We don't have to kill ourselves! I got him!'

Would he have made it back inside unaided? Impossible to say. What I do know, with sudden clarity, is that less than a year after entering our lives the 'short-arsed terrier' has burrowed into my affections in a way I wouldn't have thought possible until this relief-charged moment. We reach Lady Musgrave just after sunrise, drop anchor and flop exhausted on Trady's comfy beds. I'm almost asleep when there's a disturbance near my feet.

'Pwok,' says Lucky. ('Move over.') He burrows under the doona and executes a series of circles that end with his back fitted snugly against my chest. 'Kaark!' he says, and I couldn't agree more.

ONE

In the austere world of my New Zealand childhood, dogs seemed to have only two roles. There were the sheep and cattle workers, lean to the point of starvation, who slept on wet sacks in 44-gallon drums. Dangerous to approach, and insanely devoted to the farmers who abused them, they're as familiar now in my mind's eye (frozen in that classic half-crouch, awaiting orders) as the cows and sheep they harried about the rain-swept precipices Kiwis call hillsides.

And there were kids' dogs. Dogs that were seen but rarely contemplated. Devoted, bright-eyed mongrels that ran everywhere kids ran ... until suddenly the kids were gone and the dogs, paling at the muzzle, were left to dream and fart away their lives in the corner of a deserted bedroom.

Our dog like that was called Rusty. He was the runt of a pig-dog litter, born while my older brother, Rob, and I were staying with a fishing-and-hunting-mad Maori family over summer. Our hosts earmarked the bigger, bolder pups as future pig dogs … then gazed sadly upon their scrawny sibling, who looked like a different breed. 'That bloody foxie next door musta got to me bitch,' said the boss hunter. 'You jokers better take this rusty little fella home with you, eh?'

Rusty grew to about the size of a blue heeler. He wasn't particularly clever, or brave, or given to tricks. But he was devoted, and his presence became the one thing I could count on within our peculiar family. My parents, now long gone, fought nastily and often. Dad was a veteran of the Great War, 56 when I was born in 1951, whose experiences in the trenches led to his obsession with conspiracy theories. ('Wars don't just happen,' he'd lecture all comers. 'They're engineered by the same people who control the world's finances.' And so on.)

A widower when he met my mother, he'd been an entrepreneurial journalist and editor in Australia and New Zealand until his crusades and quick fists led him, unbowed, into isolation. Twenty years his junior, Mum was a small-town girl with no interest in politics. All she had ever hoped for was a nice home and a conventional life. Neither of them had what they wanted, and by the time Rusty joined us (when I was nine) they'd adopted separate zones: him in his 'den' churning out conspiracy exposés that would never be read; her in our spotless living room surrounded by homemaker magazines and much-repaired porcelain figurines.

When they clashed and the figurines flew, Rusty would sometimes creep into my room and hide under the bed. But mostly we ran from it: out of the house, down the hill and across the fields, the dog pacing beside me. We lived on the upper reaches of Auckland Harbour, where I found a leaky dinghy and fitted it with an oar and a blanket as a mast and sail. In this tiny deathtrap, which sailed in only one direction, Rusty and I journeyed for hours, putting ashore when hunger struck to raid an orchard or dig cockles on the mudflats.

In a way, it was the best of boyhoods. With other ragged kids, we were always in motion: climbing trees, building carts, fishing, blowing things up with gunpowder from the bullets Dad kept in the shed, and later — when we all had air-rifles — staging running battles in which we did our best to gun one another down. (In one bloody afternoon, a big Polish kid with an air-rifle the size of a bazooka managed to plug me in the ankle, Rob in the arm and Rusty in the backside. We did our own surgery with a pocket knife.)

Every so often, as though snapping out of something, our father would put aside his typewriter and build us kites, or model yachts, or organise a family picnic. He would take Rusty's head in his hands and talk to him with real interest — 'So, old mate, what do you make of that snooty new labrador across the street?' — as if he actually expected a reply. It seemed a bit odd at first, probably because I'd never seen anyone else talk to a dog, only at them.

Rusty couldn't get enough of it. He would gaze into Dad's eyes and make odd little groaning noises I'd never heard before. Yet when I tried it, Rusty just looked bored. It was years later before I understood what Dad meant about animals only reacting to 'true voices': if our inflections don't match our feelings, they ignore us.

And like most kids, the older I got the more I ignored the family dog. I remember him riding in our first bomb car, only because it was so slow and smoky he sometimes leapt from a window and ran alongside us. But I have no memory at all of what he ate, or even where he slept. And when Rob and I eventually took off to go surfing in Australia in the mid-1960s, we abandoned our trusty Rusty with barely a thought.

TWO

Not long before Lucky enters our lives in late 2000, Leisa and I — both journalists — take leave and set off on our Sail of the Century: a live-aboard cruise on *Tradewind*, the roomy old cruising trimaran we bought between us a few years earlier. For six months we roam the east coast between our home port of Brisbane and Cairns — exploring, fishing and loafing about a succession of islands, coral cays and mainland bays.

Before long, both of us are jumping out of our skins with health and happiness. For me, it's the scratching of a lifelong itch. Ever since I lay in the bottom of that leaky dinghy as a kid, watching the hills go by, the sensation of steady progress over the water under sail has thrilled me in a way I still can't explain. On Trady — well built and seaworthy — we find that even the occasional rough passage leaves an oddly physical sort of happiness (we made it!), as though some unused part of us has come into play.

But all too soon it's time to head back to Brisbane, the prospect of work and suburbia hanging like a cloud on the southern horizon. When we stop for fuel and provisions at Airlie Beach in the Whitsundays, a nondescript little mongrel greets us at the fuel wharf. While we fill the tanks, she trots up and down watching intently, as though engaged in some sort of search.

'Hello, little one,' calls Leisa. 'Are you lost?'

The dog sits, tilts her head and gives a single bark.

'That's a "yes"!' Leisa tells me. She finishes coiling the water hose, jumps onto the wharf and hoists the dog in her arms. 'Wow, check out these amazing eyelashes.' It's true: up close, the dockside urchin looks like Cleopatra with extensions. Over the next 24 hours we see 'Madam Lash' hanging out in backpacker bars, beachcombing, escorting tourists in the main street and snoozing prettily on the yacht-club lawn.

But she isn't lost, explains a man drinking wine in a park, just very nosy.

'About what?'

'Everything!' the drunk cries, waving his arms. 'That little mongrel watches everybody! It knows everything!'

We never discover who owns Lash, but her habits suggest a frustrated boat dog confined to land. We've encountered quite a few seagoing mutts in our travels, and like their owners they're an odd mix of intense sociability and fierce independence. Yet most were large animals: good for guarding boats in port, but a bit bulky and clumsy at sea. The idea of a small, portable boat dog appeals to us for the future. 'But not a silly lap-dog,' says Leisa. 'It'd have to be able to do its own thing, like little Lash.'

In the final days of the wonderful cruise we make a pact. As soon as we can afford it, we'll run away again. But not just for six months.

Next time, we'll quit our jobs and make Trady home for at least a couple of years. We'll explore the top half of coastal Australia (avoiding the cold, unpredictable southern bits), cross the Coral Sea to New Caledonia, then go island-hopping about the mighty Pacific. At anchor in the shelter of one last island, we raise our glasses to the Cruising Dream Pact of September 2000 ... never guessing how long it will take to come true.

Within weeks of our return to Brisbane, it starts to feel as if we imagined the whole adventure. Each morning, instead of lapping waves and the clink of rigging, we wake to the drone of lawnmowers and the hammerings of countless renovators: part of the accelerating gentrification of riverside Bulimba on Brisbane's inner southside. Since we left, the down-at-heel main street (a stone's throw from Leisa's old 'worker's' cottage) has been transformed into yet another café strip for urban preeners. The kerbs are lined with jellybean-like scooters and sports cars, and scores of Lycra-sheathed cyclists lounge about sucking on straws and assessing one another's bulges.

Our 'redepressing' period (as in divers decompressing) is tougher for Leisa, who has to spend her working days at *The Australian*'s Brisbane bureau. Being an out-of-state writer for Fairfax's *Good Weekend* magazine, I get to work from home ... and my first post-sail assignment is a piece about our cruise. But because I'm still *out there* in spirit, my perspective feels oddly skewed. I take long walks beside the river, trying to distil the mood, but instead find my thoughts (like Fitzgerald's famous boats against the current) 'borne back ceaselessly into the past'.

My route includes a section of riverbank where a few old slipways and boat-building yards are still holding out against the real-estate frenzies of the new era. Wedged bizarrely among these doomed relics is the little pre-fabricated house I rented after my marriage ended in the mid-1990s.

It was an aimless time when I thought about resurrecting a youthful plan of buying a boat and sailing away. But the notion seemed clichéd and past its prime, like a lot of my ideas back then. So I sat on the veranda watching other people's yachts come and go: each one a cosy, self-contained world. That winter, unusually cold and wet, my ex-wife, Lynn, sent our family's old border collie to stay with me. (Our two grown kids were off adventuring, leaving the ailing Badger home alone during Lynn's working hours.)

Once the neighbourhood speedster, Badger's back legs had become so arthritic I had to carry him outside for a pee before bed in case he fell on the steps. One awful morning, I woke about 3 am during a downpour, hearing faint cries, and found I'd left the back door open. Poor old Badger was sprawled on the flooded lawn, unable to rise. The look he gave me was unmistakeable: not recrimination, but a heartbreaking mix of embarrassment and apology. I carried him inside and dried him beside the heater, then tucked him up next to me in bed. Later that day, with Lynn's tearful agreement, I drove Badger to the family vet and had him euthanised.

The next part of my walking circuit looks across the river to the changing skyline of Teneriffe and, beyond it, Fortitude Valley — both, like Bulimba, being reworked into stamping grounds for young, cashed-up apartment dwellers.

The Valley, as locals know it, is where I met Leisa Scott during one of those outrageously long journalists' lunches that once characterised the craft.

Around 2 am, our addled lunch crowd ended up in some sort of bikie bar where 'Scotty' outed herself as one of perhaps ten people in the world who'd read a novel I'd written years earlier.

'Flaming dogs,' she kept babbling. 'Your book had a flaming dog falling from the sky! And me too ...' — pointing at herself — '... I had a flaming dog! Poor Tasha. The cane went up — whoosh! — and her ears came off ...' (It was weeks before we completed that chat: my fictional dog, plucked, still smoking, from a bushfire by a man dangling from a helicopter, bites his rescuer causing both to fall to their deaths. Leisa's childhood pet was caught in a cane-farm burn, but survived minus her ears.)

From the start, I fell for Scotty's gutsy style: the way she tore into a tattooed giant who tried to steal her chair at that post-lunch bikie bar; her outrageous description of watching a hookworm emerge from her own foot in Zanzibar during a six-month solo trek through Africa; her sartorial eccentricities and disdain for 'girlie' preoccupations like shopping ... and, of course, her exquisite taste in obscure first novels.

As a kid, too young to hang out with her older sisters, Leisa was left to her own devices on the family cane farm at Gooburrum, near Bundaberg, where almost nothing happened. Like me in my leaky dinghy, she spent entire days on her bike, pedalling the flat, dusty roads between avenues of cane while imagining adventures in exotic places. 'So long as I was moving,' she told me, 'it felt like I was already on my way to those places. I started to think of the local roads as a maze, and that one day I'd find one leading out of there to the life I imagined.'

That road turned out to be journalism. At 17, Leisa was transported from her sheltered life as a 'good little Lutheran' to a cadetship on

The Courier-Mail in Brisbane. It was 1984, the final stages of the old, hard-drinking journalistic era, and Scotty — thrilled by the humour, ideas and camaraderie — was soon propping up bars with the wildest of the old-school mavericks. And though she later travelled extensively, worked abroad and completed a university degree, she never really adjusted to the bland, corporate-think types who began taking over the world's newsrooms in the 1990s.

The final leg of my writer's block tour passes Bulimba's original café, where Scotty and I became regulars. It was here, over numerous glasses of red, that we first talked of buying a boat. (We'd already had an overnight sail on a friend's yacht. It was unexpectedly rough, yet the landlubber from Bundaberg showed no hint of illness and stunned our seasoned skipper by declaring the experience 'relaxing'.)

A couple of years later, in 1997, we became joint owners of *Tradewind*, a 12-metre Piver design trimaran built in 1983. It's not a flash boat. There's none of the state-of-the-art gadgetry found on modern production yachts, and the construction is marine ply with fibreglass sheathing, which needs regular maintenance. But apart from being much cheaper ($50,000) than similar-sized catamarans (which start around $250,000), and roomier than monohulls, it's ideal for cruising the reef, with shallow draught and the ability to sit evenly aground, unlike deep-keeled boats and many old-style journalists.

THREE

On a morning when I'm close to finishing the cruising story, Scotty phones from work.

'A little dog is on death row.'

'Huh?'

'Someone left him at the vet's in Cooroy,' she says. 'If he doesn't get a home in a week or so they'll have to put him down. Mim's mum says he has legs like a cabriole chair.' Mim is one of Leisa's workmates. Mim's mum — uniquely qualified to comment — is a small-dog lover and antique dealer with a store opposite the Cooroy Veterinary Clinic on the Sunshine Coast.

Could this be our sea dog? That night, we hit the veranda to consider our options. So far, all we know about 'Lucky' is that he's some sort of small, furry terrier-cross, about 18 months old, left at the clinic two months earlier suffering tick paralysis. Wildly unkempt, he also had pneumonia and was vomiting and producing a 'green' discharge. The vet shaved off his neglected coat and removed the tick that was killing him, then castrated him and waited for his owners to return.

They never came. Normally, with so many dogs needing homes, that would have been the end for Lucky. But the vet's young assistant, Suzanne, took a shine to him. 'He's a bit special,' she told us by phone. 'You know how some dogs just really connect with you? Lucky's one of those.'

Suzanne already has three dogs and can't keep Lucky permanently: 'But I wasn't going to let anything happen to him if I could help it, so he's been spending nights at my place and days at the clinic.'

The portents seem right. We need something to pull us out of our post-cruise blues, Suzanne needs to offload a house guest, and Lucky — having clawed his way back from the edge — needs another chance at life. We'll have to upgrade the backyard fence, but that's easy. The only unknown is how he'll take to the boat. It'll be several years before we can afford to take off on our extended, live-aboard cruise, but there'll be plenty of weekend and holiday sails in the meantime for Lucky to gain his sea legs.

'What if he hates it?' worries Scotty. 'What if he craps and vomits everywhere, like that poor bloody poodle we saw at Magnetic Island?' (Press-ganged aboard a Victorian millionaire's luxury catamaran, the delicate lap-dog owned by the millionaire's trophy wife suffered daily bouts of appalling incontinence.)

But the timing of Lucky's plight — only weeks after little Madam Lash planted the seed at Airlie Beach — seems so serendipitous we know we have to go with it. 'To Lucky!' we toast. 'To adventures with mysterious terriers!'

Next day I call Suzanne at the clinic and agree to take her foundling sight unseen. On a Saturday morning in late October 2000, we set off up the Bruce Highway to collect our Lucky dip. The little hamlet of Cooroy, bypassed by the highway years earlier, is only 25 kilometres from Noosa Heads yet there's barely a soul on the streets when we reach the clinic around noon.

We've just begun our introductions in the waiting room when a flurry of clicking paws heralds Lucky's arrival in a doorway leading to the surgery. Still close-cropped from his recent treatment, he's very short with floppy ears, a black button nose and a tail that curls into a rigid circle. He moves his large eyes quite deliberately from one of us to the other, then — with much wiggling and tail wagging — hurries into the room and greets us like old friends.

Scotty scoops him up and holds him, marvelling at the softness of his creamy brown fur. 'Kik!' he snorts after a few moments repose, and we know instantly this means, 'Enough! Put me down!'

While we do his paperwork, Lucky bustles about as if born here: welcoming a new dog patient, inspecting the display of pet food and toys, and growling mightily at a cat he spots being whisked out the back of the surgery. Finally, with Suzanne and Lucky, we stroll to the car. I open the back door and place Lucky's worldly belongings (a leash, certificates of sterilisation and vaccination, and our gift of a stuffed zebra) on the seat.

'In you go, mate.'

He stares up at me, then turns and looks quizzically at Suzanne.

'Farewell, little Lucky,' she says. 'Have a great life.'

He jumps in and settles on the back seat.

Driving away, we speculate about where among the surrounding wooded hillsides, with their many rough bush acreages and hobby farms, he may have grown up. All we know of his former owners is that they were locals, but from what Suzanne has told us of Lucky hurling himself at her larger dogs during mealtime disputes it seems likely he was a bush mutt whose life so far has been an exercise in survival.

After only a few minutes, Lucky clambers through from the back seat and stands on Scotty's lap with his front paws on the dashboard, as though seeking a clue as to where the fates might be sending him now.

Then he turns, gives one of his snorts and begins scaling her chest. He climbs onto her left shoulder, shimmies along the back of her neck like a self-adjusting stole, lowers his chin onto her right shoulder and closes his eyes. He's still there 15 minutes later when I notice Scotty wiping her eyes.

'What's wrong?'

'Nothing. It's just …' She turns, holding Lucky's vaccination papers.

'He's just so little and alone. And all the things he's done, his whole life so far, is gone. All that's left is this.' She reads from the papers: 'Breed: terrier x. Colour: cream. Weight: five kilograms …' Scotty presses her face against the dog's neck. 'Five kilograms,' she whispers in his ear. 'How the hell can anything weigh five kilograms?'

Lucky lifts his head and gives her a look. 'Kik!' he says, meaning, 'Enough! Quit fussing!'

FOUR

Lucky's background isn't lost to him, but for us his settling-in period is like watching an exotic bud unfurl its secrets. A few days after he arrives, we're playing with him on the floor when he suddenly starts to buzz like an electronic toy. It's an amazing noise from deep in his throat that's unlike anything we've heard from a dog: primitive and joyous and strangely amplified, a bit like the throat-singing of Inuit women.

At first, Lucky turns on his Love Buzz only during rough-house sessions. He rears up, seizes you with his cabriole legs — which seem to have an extra joint — and buzzes. It's like being hugged by a living teddy bear. (After a while, all that's needed to trigger a buzz is to ruffle the side of his head.) He doesn't have hair but incredibly soft fur that never moults or smells, and he adopts a curious torpedo-like relaxing position: belly-down, with front legs folded into a natural muff and the rear ones comically splayed, like the fins of a missile.

But there's a side to our mystery mutt in direct contrast to his sociability: a wild side. Even for a terrier, Lucky is the most explosive, cat-chasing, lawnmower-hating little son of a bitch who ever moved in next door to an unsuspecting old suburban woman. In his defence, our neighbour's arrogant, bird-murdering cat had it coming. The first morning Lucky spots it, the pampered feline is sitting regally on our back lawn licking feathers from its paws.

An instant later, snarling like a beast from hell, our little marauder is down the stairs and after it. The cat leaps the fence; Lucky bores straight through it (more repairs needed), driving his outraged quarry under its owner's house (crash, bang!), then out again and several times around the yard; then through another neighbour's fence, and another, and another.

By the time we catch up a block away, he's chased the cat up some fire stairs to the third level of an apartment block and is working the corridors with his nose to find where it's hiding.

As I cart him home under one arm, Lucky is rigid with fury. His eyes are locked on the receding building and a low, just-you-wait growl rumbles through his chest. This turns out to be no idle threat: almost every morning, he finds a way to breach the fence repairs and scare the shit out of the old lady's cat. Already peeved about the gentrification of Bulimba (or the 'invasion of the coffee slurpers' as she calls it), our neighbour can't get her head around the idea that free-range cats are more of a menace than stroppy little dogs.

'Lock him up!' she insists.

'But if your cat wasn't hunting in our yard, he wouldn't chase it,' we argue. (This isn't strictly true. Lucky's hatred of the cat is such that he comes to learn its movements about the street and ambushes it at every chance.)

Not everyone disapproves. A retired farmer on the other side of the street monitors Lucky's pursuit of the cat with raucous glee.

'That's a dog with real dog instincts,' he tells me one morning after cheering another epic chase from his veranda. 'See the way he scratches up the ground after piddling? Most dogs don't do that any more 'cause it's domesticated out of them. So is chasing cats. I mean, what sorta dog wants to be friends with a bloody cat!'

Indeed. But the animal Lucky most wants to be friends with — my son Nick's much-admired kelpie-cross — treats him with contempt. Lucky is overcome with love for the jet-black, yellow-eyed Jake, whose hauteur reflects his status as that ultimate Aussie mutt: the untethered ute dog. Alas, Jake's response is to either ignore Lucky or torment him in various fiendish ways.

It starts when Nick and I take both dogs to a nearby open space for a run. Lucky tries to keep up with his new hero, but Jake sprints far ahead. Then he turns and hurtles back towards Lucky, occasionally veering aside at the last moment but more often sending him flying with a blow from his muscular shoulder. Lucky keeps getting up, but after a while he's reduced to turning in anxious circles in an effort to gauge the angle of Jake's next assault. He glances my way a few times, but makes no sound.

As Jake lines up for another charge, something that feels like a paternal instinct spurts through my veins. Actually, it's more complicated than that. I can tell my 24-year-old son is enjoying Jake's sport with the 'lap-dog', and that his enjoyment is linked to our own young-bull–old-bull status. So I move closer to Lucky and wait. Tongue lolling, Jake pounds in for the metaphoric kill. At the last moment, I interpose a leg so that instead of barrelling Lucky the kelpie hits my knee and drops winded to the ground.

'What's wrong with Jake?' calls Nick, who missed the manoeuvre.

'Fell over,' I tell him.

But Lucky knows what happened. 'Kaark!' he says, moving even closer to my legs. Unnecessarily, as it turns out, because Jake — though on his feet in seconds — has lost interest in the game. But he never grows tired of finding new ways to make Lucky squirm. His cruellest trick involves the stuffed zebra toy that has become Lucky's pride and joy.

Over several visits to the house, Jake watches Lucky throwing the ragged thing about and trying to inveigle people into tug-of-war games with it. (At night, he carries it into the little fruit crate he sleeps in at the end of our bed and uses it as a pillow.)

Jake, of course, isn't a stuffed-toy sort of dog. He's been around Australia on the back of a ute, hung out on building sites with tradesmen, and fought awful battles with the sort of scary mongrels that appear in pig-hunting magazines. Yet one night, when Nick, Jake and others arrive for dinner and Lucky fusses excitedly over his idol, Jake ignores him and goes straight for the stuffed zebra. He picks it up and saunters about the house, watching for a reaction from the corner of those knowing yellow eyes.

Sure enough, Lucky eventually goes bonkers. Snarling and baring his tiny white teeth, he rushes his tormentor repeatedly … but they're only feints, and when his courage finally deserts him, Lucky, trembling with fear and embarrassment, goes into torpedo mode behind an armchair and won't be consoled. Jake resumes his victory parade with the stuffed toy. Most guests think it's hilarious, but Scotty and I are secretly outraged. We long to rip the zebra from Jake's taunting jaws, but even as we discuss this furtively in the kitchen, we have to laugh at the absurdity of the impulse.

After only a few weeks under his influence, we're on the verge of allowing ourselves to become extensions of Lucky's formidable will.

'It's not his fault he's so lovable,' says Scotty when the guests have gone. We're sitting on the end of the bed, watching him staring up from his little box. (The moment Jake left, Lucky retrieved his drool-soaked zebra and slunk off to bed.)

'You're right,' I tell her. 'And Jake is an evil, manipulative genius. But if we keep fighting Lucky's battles for him, we could end up regretting it.'

'Why? He's so little. How could he ever get his zebra back from the likes of Jake? We should have helped him. I could *feel* him pleading for help, couldn't you?'

I nod. 'Actually, he asked me outright, when I went inside during dessert, to kick Jake's gigantic nuts into next week. And now — are you getting it? — he's asking if we can waive our rule and let him sleep up here tonight ...'

With a whoop, Scotty hoists the mind-controlling terrier onto the bed. 'Kaark!' he rejoices, rolling onto his back and raising his legs like victory flags.

Soon afterwards, while we're driving to the Hunter Valley to spend a weekend with friends, Lucky disappears. One moment he's there (perched on his usual vantage point atop the back seat), the next he isn't. Leisa checks the floor behind our seats. No Lucky. She drags herself across the back seat and looks among the bags in the wagon's luggage compartment. Nothing.

'But I saw him!' I tell her. 'Just minutes ago, in the rear-vision mirror. He was wedged up there between the back headrests.'

Leisa does another search. 'Jesus,' she says, resuming her seat. 'This is getting weird. Let's pull over.'

We stop and pile everything from the back seat onto the ground. Still no Lucky. Dry mouthed, I open the rear gate to check the luggage section. 'If he's not in here,' I tell Scotty, 'we'll have to check in somewhere for a lot of therapy.' As I move the nearest travel bag, a fluffy little head pops out of its unzipped top. 'Lucky!' we chorus, dragging him out for a hug.

'Kik!' he grumbles. He struggles free and burrows back into the bag until all we can see is the tip of an ear.

Driving on into the dusk, an idea presents itself. We've booked a motel at Armidale to break the journey, intending to let Lucky sleep in the car. But what if he just happened to be in the bag when it was carried to the unit? Footballers and rock stars are allowed in motels, and unlike them Lucky is reliably house-trained, doesn't moult or smell, and has never trashed a room in his life. 'Fantastic,' says Scotty. 'Let's do it.'

We park a discreet distance from the motel office and leave Lucky in the car while we check in. That's when I notice the proprietor's cat and decide on a small change of plan to allow for the possibility that Lucky might, at some stage during the night, bark. Without warning Scotty, I feign the merest hint of

Tourette's. (Just two quick yips and a muffled obscenity, then a couple of violent head shakes to signify snapping out of something, followed by an apologetic smile.)

'Sorry darling,' I croon, smacking my lips and taking the little milk jugs from my wide-eyed partner. 'It must be starting up again.'

As soon as we're out the door, the proprietor locks it and turns off the light. Lucky doesn't make a sound all night, and obligingly hops back into the travel bag for our early morning departure. It's only after stopping at a nearby park for a walk that we realise his flash leather leash has been left behind … on the motel bed.

Scotty can't believe I want to go back: 'Didn't you *see* that man's face when you barked? He'll have the cops there by now, running tests on the leash. If you go back, they'll throw you in the pound and cut your nuts off.'

We drive on.

Our friends Col and Anne have quit the media, left Sydney and bought a small acreage near Singleton in the Hunter Valley. Both farm kids, they've reverted in middle age to their rural roots — planting trees, chopping wood, building fences and applying their seasoned palates to a rigorous testing of local wines. On this weekend, dozens of guests have come from the big smoke for Col's 50th birthday.

As we arrive, Lucky springs from his travel bag to growl ominously at a couple of cows by the driveway. Farmer Col emerges from behind a tractor and cautions us to keep an eye on our 'fluff ball' around his two big working dogs, Spud and Murphy. Which we do ... for an hour or two, until the party cranks up. By then, like everyone else, Lucky and the farm dogs seem to be getting on famously.

But late in the afternoon a terrible commotion issues from Spud and Murphy's kennel area behind the farmhouse. As one, a great mob of drunks rushes to prevent what everyone imagines is Lucky's imminent demise. We round the corner and stop, confused: the fluff ball is attacking the farm dogs! He's taken over their entire collection of weathered bones, and each time one of them tries to get close, Lucky charges — snarling and leaping at its throat until it backs off.

Spud and Murphy have clearly never encountered anything this crazy, and are at a loss. Stung by the sudden appearance of so many cheering witnesses, they join forces and advance again, teeth bared. Lucky drops the bone he's been gnawing and goes for them. His ferocity this time is so over the top that both dogs turn and run. He pursues them briefly, then toddles back and flops down amid the bones to yet another huge cheer.

After that, we know for sure: five kilograms or not, this was a mutt that grew up fighting for his supper.

FIVE

Lucky's first sail on *Tradewind* comes about a month after he joins us. By then he'd already checked out the trimaran at her berth near Bulimba, poking through all the nooks and crannies while we did a few jobs below decks, then showing his nous by heading outside and settling precisely in the shadow of the mast ... the only shade available on that blazing spring day.

But how will he go when the boat's in motion? Now that we've committed ourselves, it'd be a disaster if sickness or confinement phobia ruled him out as a sailor. His shakedown passage is a four-hour sail across Moreton Bay to Moreton Island, returning the next day.

From the moment the sails are raised — and Lucky scuttles forward to watch the bow slicing through a small chop, then turns to us with a big, windblown grin — we know our worries are over.

'Yahoo!' yells Scotty, shadowing him about the deck in case of mishaps. 'He loves it!'

But there's a catch: he loves remote beaches even more. And once he lands on one, getting him back in the dinghy before he's ready can be pretty well impossible. For the first year or so, during a succession of weekend cruises in Moreton Bay, it's a twice-daily dilemma — complicated by prowling 'wildlife' rangers whose lives are given over to official Australia's remorseless war on dogs.

A typical morning beach-run goes like this: awake at anchor off the magical western shore of Moreton Island. Hear the clickclickclickclick of Lucky patrolling on deck, and his outraged growls when he spots a dolphin or dugong or some other watery monster tolerated by people — but which, in his opinion, SHOULD NOT EXIST.

Fight urge to return to sleep because beach-runs must be early, before appearance of generally late-rising rangers. Wake notoriously late-rising Scotty and go on deck, where Lucky shows his impatience by rearing on hind legs and pawing air like tiny stallion. Scan beach with binoculars for insomniac rangers before heading ashore in dinghy, with Lucky perched on very tip of bow so as to arrive first.

Stroll along icing-sugar beach; watch Lucky run and leap for joy, bark wildly at sinister, half-submerged logs, retrieve sticks and float blissfully in the shallows. Collect his crap in plastic bags. Occasionally see glint of distant vehicle approaching along beach (the island has no sealed roads, and like thousands of tourists the rangers travel everywhere in dune-ripping four-wheel drives) and run to hide in undergrowth. Somehow, Lucky understands the urgency and huddles close.

If it is a ranger, he might spot the tiny dog prints and get out, as we watch, to investigate — sometimes standing amid rubbish left by yesterday's tourists while glaring about for the prohibited animal. If he keeps going, it means he's bound for a resort just south of the anchorage to stock up on beer and videos, and it won't be long before he's back.

So … jog back to dinghy, pull bow into water and turn imploringly to dog.

'Lucky!' — clicking fingers over dinghy — 'In you get, mate! Quickly now!'

He backs off, growling.

'Lucky! The ranger will get you. *Please*!'

Dog rushes forward, leaps in air and does slam-kick off my thigh.

'You little bastard!'

I try a flying tackle but he dodges me easily, then belts off on a series of high-speed circles, growling and swerving with each taunting pass. Okay: get in boat, start motor and pretend to abandon him. He watches for a moment, head cocked, then trots off in opposite direction.

'Let me try,' says Scotty, now almost awake.

Back to beach. Scotty crouches by boat and employs her most endearing tones. 'Come on, my darling little boy. Ohh, he's the sweetest, nicest, little darling dog. Ohh, yes he is! Here he comes now. What a clever, clever boy!' Seizing her semi-hypnotised quarry, she dunks his feet to get the sand off and drops him in the dinghy. 'I hate using that stupid baby talk,' she yells over the motor. 'But Lucky seems to go for it.' And that's it … until dusk, when rangers are usually sluggish and housebound, and we run the gauntlet again.

Lucky's contrariness at this stage isn't confined to dinghies. He's equally opposed to being put back on the leash after morning runs in our local park. With one telling difference: on beaches, he doesn't try to run away — only to prolong the experience. In the park, his sporadic rebellions are more worrying. When it's time to go back on the leash for the walk home, Lucky pauses, shoots us a calculating look, then — always with the same jaunty skip — sets off in the other direction.

The heartbreaking thing is that we can tell the little ingrate means it. He is leaving forever, trotting purposefully away down unknown streets without a backward glance. Yet when we run after him, or intercept him several blocks away in the car, he acts as though nothing has happened. These proofs of our unrequited love start to really get to me. 'Piss off then, you buzzing runt!' I scream after him one morning. 'No wonder your owners dumped you!'

Disciplinarian dog owners watch these antics knowingly, and never fail to offer advice about choke chains, or mental conditioning, or showing a dog who's boss. In some ways, of course, they're right: in any urban setting, people who can't control their dogs are courting tragedy. But Scotty and I grew up in places where dogs ran free and developed to their potential. Just like people, some became smart, high-spirited and humorous, some worthy and serious, others dull and sullen. (And, yes disciplinarians, some got run over.)

Our problem with punishment-based training, even in suburbia, is that it seems to reliably transform smart and lively dogs into boring ones — a fate we won't inflict on the irrepressible Lucky. Our hope is that through trust and friendship we'll eventually win him over. At this stage, though, we're floundering. For a while, in desperation, we tried using angry tones and even smacks on the bum after his bolting episodes. But this just made him more intransigent and left us feeling treacherous: in our frustration, we were widening the rift rather than healing it.

Yet if mechanical obedience born of punishment remains the only measure of a 'good' dog, we'll take our chances with a so-called bad one. Already there are hopeful signs for the future. The last time Lucky sought to do a bunk from the park, Scotty lured him back with the same sweet baby tones she used to get him into the dinghy. (Which raises two possibilities: either my father was wrong about animals responding only to 'true voices', or Scotty's true voice is that of a charismatic infant.)

Another development: if we risk a fine and leave the hated leash at home, Lucky follows us without fuss, even when it's time to leave the park. We're starting to think his leash phobia, and his boundless delight in freedom, may both stem from him having been tied up and ignored for long periods, a common fate among bush dogs with itchy feet.

SIX

Lucky falls off Trady only once, under full sail in Moreton Bay. 'Dog overboard!' cries Nick, who sees him overbalance while growling at water surging between the hulls. We're belting along at 10 knots with a following wind, and by the time we furl the headsail and come about our 'Little Buoy' is a speck in the distance. Closing in, we can see he's paddling towards us so desperately half his body is out of the water. On our first pass, Nick manages to grab him by a leg and heave him onto the deck.

Furious with himself ('Kaar!'), he lets Scotty towel him off then goes below and doesn't emerge for hours. That slip-up aside, his balance is surpassed only by his astonishing bladder control. One morning, after 15 hours without landfall, I watch him shuffle along the pitching deck until he's next to a side stay, then lift a leg and wedge it against the stay before letting rip non-stop for almost a minute — directly into the sea.

Eight months after joining us, Lucky makes his first extended cruise to Gladstone, 306 nautical miles from Brisbane. With two mates as crew, we set off while Scotty is in journalistic mode far to the north, doing a leg on a tall ship during its circumnavigation of Australia. The plan is that she'll leave the sailing ship at Weipa in the Gulf of Carpentaria, then fly to Gladstone to join me and Lucky for the sail home.

She's upset about missing the sea dog's inaugural blue-water cruise, but the timing can't be avoided. Scotty promises to keep in touch by satellite phone, and — mindful of Lucky's recent topple into Moreton Bay — makes me promise never to let him on deck while we're under way.

The first half of the voyage is calm and uneventful: up the coast past Noosa Heads to Double Island Point, then across the often dangerous Wide Bay bar at the southern end of Fraser Island and through the Great Sandy Straits to Hervey Bay.

We loaf for a couple of days in a beautiful tidal lagoon on the northwestern tip of Fraser Island, then leave on a mid-afternoon tide for the 80 nautical mile leg to Lady Musgrave Island. Our course, almost due north, threads between a series of cays and islands that form the southern extremity of the Great Barrier Reef — picturesque by day, but scary on an inky, moonless night when thoughts of boat-wrecking submerged reefs tend to run wild.

By 11 pm the wind, forecast at 15–20 knots, is gusting to 30 and over.

That's when the cross-sea develops, throwing Lucky repeatedly off the sofa and leading to his amazing trick of using a cushion as a body wedge. He's been a little trooper the whole trip: no sea sickness, fastidiously clean, and content to curl up in a corner for hours when conditions demand our full attention.

The cushion trick shows for the first time the true extent of his intelligence and ingenuity. This isn't just a promising boat dog, I boast to my mate Des as we rocket on through the night, this is a *born sailor*! It's about an hour later when I notice Lucky is missing from the sofa, and that the sliding cabin door is half-open. (Months later, Lucky demonstrates that the door only needs to be left open a few centimetres for him to get his nose into the crack and force it apart.)

In the heady moments after I pluck Lucky from the edge of the deck (or oblivion, as it would surely have been had he fallen), Des watches me towel him dry on the sofa. 'You know,' he points out, 'another dog busting for a leak would probably have just done it in the cabin.' Which is true. But Lucky never has: not on the boat, or at home. And on the few occasions when he's been forced to crap on the deck, he does it right at the seaward edge where it's easy to nudge overboard.

But the most telling thing about Lucky to emerge from the boys-only cruise is his uncanny sense of ... well, us. The closer people get to him, the more he's able to read our moods, anticipate our movements, and even share our jokes. Since we left Brisbane, Lucky and a journo friend, Adrian, have tussled daily for possession of the sofa, which Lucky considers his. On our second morning at anchor in the lagoon at Lady Musgrave, Adrian comes in from a swim to find the short-arsed terrier has beaten him to the prize.

Adrian knows Lucky is compelled to rush to the stern when the diesel is started (to bark and rage at the gushing exhaust outlet ... thus letting me know the cooling system is working), and that his cue for this is a hand extended towards the ignition key. So Adrian touches the key.

In a flash, Lucky is out the door and ready to rumble. Moments later, he pokes his head back in to see what's causing the delay. By then Adrian is stretched out on the sofa with a novel.

'Ha, ha!' he crows. 'Tricked ya!'

Lucky bounds in and leaps on top of him, growling and buzzing in delighted recognition of the joke. They wrestle a little before reaching a compromise and taking a nap side by side.

The following day we're entering an isolated tidal creek near Gladstone to anchor for the night when I make a blunder that almost puts us on the rocks. As soon as we realise we're on the wrong side of the entrance, Lucky (reading the change in our voices) alights beside me on the helmsman's seat. I swing hard right towards deeper water, but by then jagged boulders are visible just below the keel.

'Stop! Stop!' shrieks Adrian.

'Back up!' yells Des.

'Ka-ka-ka!' ('What gives?!!') snorts Lucky, prodding my arm with a paw. (His expression, when I glance down, is a study in transferred alarm.)

I ignore them all. With several knots of incoming tide behind us, trying to stop or back up would spin the wide, difficult-to-reverse tri out of control. Our best chance is to motor on across the current towards the *real* channel, hoping Trady's shallow (0.9 metre) draught will get us through. The final few hundred metres are a torment, with ever nastier rocks ahead.

As we pass miraculously over each clump (the others tell me later), I actually rise from the seat, teeth clenched, then lower again. And when I rise and lower, so does Lucky.

'It was hilarious,' hoots Des, an ex-TV news boss, when we're safely at anchor. 'The only thing you were doing that Lucky wasn't doing was sweating like a doomed pig.'

SEVEN

From Gladstone, Des and Adrian fly back to Brisbane, while Lucky and I kick back at the local marina. In a few days, Scotty will arrive for the passage home, which gives me time to reprovision, repair a leak in the dinghy and explore the waterfront. Somehow, Lucky knows we're waiting for his favourite woman. While I potter, he spends hours in torpedo mode atop the cabin, monitoring every movement along our section of the marina.

Scotty has been reporting for her newspaper from the tall ship that is replicating Matthew Flinders' circumnavigation. It's a quirky little venture: in her last phone call during a stopover at Thursday Island in the Torres Strait, Scotty told of bumping into the skipper — a one-time navy man who was then in the process of undergoing a sex change — outside the island's beauty parlour, where she (the skipper) was awaiting a bikini wax.

The spartan, alcohol-free vessel carries paying guests who double as rope pullers, and a regular crew of earnest young volunteers with a shared Bligh complex.

'Buy lots of booze and food!' Scotty urged. 'These boring little rule freaks are wearing me down.'

When Scotty arrives, Trady's ample food-storage areas are packed to capacity. The fridge and freezer are full of exotic goodies and vacuum-sealed meats (including Lucky's favourite, raw chicken wings), and the bulging fruit and vegetable hammock is making the galley smell like a greengrocery.

Even by our standards, it's a power of tucker. We leave on a morning tide and anchor that afternoon at Pancake Creek, a snug little hideaway tucked in behind Bustard Head, 30 nautical miles east-southeast of Gladstone, and sheltered from most winds. Which is just as well: early the next morning, a sou'easterly buster roars in at 40 knots, and despite the protective headland sets up a fiendish howl through the rigging of the four boats straining at anchor along a bend in the creek.

By the afternoon, chilly rain is blasting sideways across the landscape. Based on the forecast it'll be some time before we can continue south. For the next few days, while the squalls intensify, Trady becomes the sort of restaurant old-style journalists dream about. A restaurant whose bar never closes; where smoking, strong language and controversy are welcome, and hearty, slow-cooked meals (osso bucco, curries, Texas-style chilli) are the order of the day.

Twice daily, we struggle into wet-weather gear and ferry Lucky ashore for his toilet breaks. If it's really bucketing down, we take him to a sandbank nearer the boat where he belts up and down through the soft sand, putting up pelicans and dancing delightedly among swirling armies of soldier crabs.

Around midnight on the fifth day of the blow, we're jerked awake by the bloodcurdling sounds of a pitched dingo fight on the beach.

Lucky explodes, snarling and bouncing off the cabin walls as though desperate to get in there and sort them out. In the morning, enormous paw prints are visible on the sand: not real dingoes, but the sort of hybridised wild dogs now haunting the fringes of developed Australia. One sniff of the tracks is enough to demoralise last night's tough-talking sea dog.

'Pffft!' he snorts ('No!'), and jerks back as though scalded. His ears and tail droop and he presses close to my legs, staying there until it's time to leave. Getting Lucky off beaches has become progressively easier, and on this morning he's back in the dinghy and waiting before it's even launched. But the moment we're under way he's up on the gunwale barking and bad-mouthing any feral dogs still within earshot.

Around this time we begin to recognise the extent of Lucky's mind games. He's a fantasist, a four-legged Walter Mitty, forever tricking himself into believing in dangers and challenges that don't exist, then fearlessly confronting his own phantoms. Half-submerged logs are lurking monsters (no matter how often he confirms their status as logs); men on pushbikes are demons who must be growled at (but only from a passing car: if he's on foot, they're just men on bikes); all fish are murderous boat invaders that must be kept at bay (unless caught and on deck, when they're of no interest).

Just when we think all dangers perceived by Lucky are imaginary, up pops a dog-who-cried-wolf twist. As we follow the bush line along an empty beach on the other side of the headland, he suddenly darts at our ankles, snapping and growling.

'What is it now?' I yell. 'Zombie mermaids? Giant, killer crayfish? Outta the way, you fraud!' Lucky spreads his legs, looks directly into my eyes and barks defiantly. We keep walking, even when his barks take on a frenzied edge.

'Watch it!' cries Scotty, grabbing my arm. And there, just ahead, is a big black snake. It's coiled atop the line of high-tide flotsam we've been shuffling through with bare feet, and as we stand there — urging the still yapping Lucky to keep back — it exits slowly into the bush.

'Good boy!' we chorus then, but our Mitty mutt flicks us an injured look and trots off.

(He goes through the same routine not long afterwards, while we're walking in Bulimba. Wary this time, I find a recently shed snakeskin in some weeds a few metres away.)

It's ten days before the big blow finally subsides and the seas diminish. By then, the weather has claimed two yachts attempting to shelter in the scant protection of Lady Musgrave's lagoon, just 25 nautical miles to our east. (On the VHF radio, we heard of the crews being lifted off by chopper before their yachts were driven onto the encircling reef and wrecked.) It's another lesson for the future: the lagoon is a great fair-weather haven, but in sustained blows over 20 knots it becomes one of the world's most beautiful traps.

With our mountain of supplies almost gone, we chug out of Pancake Creek at sunrise then raise the sails and follow the coastline south. The next few days are idyllic: electric blue skies, a following breeze of around 10 knots, and a series of dolphin escorts working the bow. With Trady on autopilot, there's little to do but lie back on deck and watch the shoreline unfold at a steady 5–6 knots.

Conditions are so gentle we suspend our rule and allow Lucky on deck while we're under way. Off Bundaberg, I wake from a nap in a beanbag and find him draped about my head, snoring gently, his cheek against mine. When I speak to him, he turns his head and applies a single delicate lick to the tip of my nose. 'Kaark!' he says, stretching mightily, and nods off again. And so it goes until we enter the Great Sandy Straits between Fraser Island and the mainland, when the skies darken ahead of another southerly blow.

It's the sort of lousy timing that plagues all boaties on a schedule: in another 12 hours, we'll be through the shallow, winding straits and ready to cross the notorious Wide Bay bar near Fraser Island's southern tip. But if there is another big blow it could be days before the swell drops enough for us to tackle the bar and complete the last leg home. We anchor that night at Pelican Bay, just inside the bar entrance, and spread out the charts and cruising guides.

The southerly is already blowing, but still under 20 knots. If it doesn't rise too much overnight, we could cross the bar on the morning's rising tide and shelter behind nearby

Double Island Point until the unfavourable wind subsides. That way, we won't be trapped inside the straits if bar conditions progressively worsen, meaning further delays.

As we lay plans, Lucky jumps onto the table and appears to study the charts. He listens anxiously to Scotty's main concern (what if the swell's already too big for a safe crossing?), then turns to hear my reassurances, then — mollified by the positive tone — turns back to Scotty with a look that seems to say: 'Are we okay with that?' (A month at sea has honed his people-interpreting skills to the point where it's almost impossible to have a conversation without him.)

Next morning we turn on the VHF to find a desperate little drama unfolding on the bar we're due to cross in less than an hour. It starts when a lone sailor calls the local volunteer coastguard to report that he's about to enter the bar from the open sea. He has no GPS or charts, and so can't follow the usual co-ordinates to avoid the bar's dangerous breaking areas. His small yacht is powered only by an outboard motor, and his radio manner is unorthodox.

'Aw, fuck it,' he drawls. 'I'm just gunna go for it!'

Despite repeated calls from the coastguard, nothing more is heard from him for about ten minutes. Then he's back, screaming over the wind static: 'Oh no! Oh Jesus, they're too big! I'm fucked, I'm gorn!' Then nothing.

'Just stay calm,' the English-accented coastguard keeps saying, 'and hold your course. When you get inside, you can make a nice cup of tea.'

Another burst of static, then: '... cuppa tea be fucked! I'm fuckin' history! Oh Jesus, here we go ...' Then he's gone again.

Scotty and Lucky sit side by side across the table staring at me — the one who wants to take them out where the screaming happens. For a moment, it looks as though both of them have dramatically raised right eyebrows (which almost makes *me* scream), but when I blink and look again, it's only Scotty.

'Are we quite sure about this?' she asks.

'Kuk!' ('Be honest!') snorts Lucky.

'Of course,' I lie. 'Let's get moving before we miss the tide.'

When we're under way, Scotty calls the coastguard to give the usual notice from a vessel about to cross the bar. The radio operator tells her the swell is moderate, but that a couple of trawlers, which crossed earlier, reported some big sets 'standing up' along the bar's outer rim. There's no mention of the lone sailor.

Rounding the point minutes later, we see him puttering towards us. The little yacht is a mess, with ropes and sails trailing in the water and a list that suggests a flooded bilge. As we watch, the lone sailor ducks low in his cockpit. At the same moment our radio crackles: '*Tradewind, Tradewind*!'

It's him! Before Scotty can respond, the desperate voice rushes on: 'Don't go out there, *Tradewind*! It's a fucking nightmare! Huge fucking waves everywhere! I repeat: abort, abort!'

Abort, abort?

Scotty gives me a wide-eyed look, but betrays nothing with her diplomatic response: '*Shrieker, Shrieker* [not its real name], this is *Tradewind*. Thanks for your concern, but we have a GPS so it'll be a lot easier for us. Good to see you made it through, over.'

A pause, then: '. . . GPS be fucked! I'm talking green walls, lady. Don't fuckin' do it!' By this time he's passed only 20 metres from us and is gesturing dramatically at our receding stern. Ahead lies a part of the inner-bar known as the Washing Machine — not breaking waves, but a turbulent confluence of chop and current along the edge of a long sandy shoal.

Although we've crossed the bar several times before, the lone sailor's ravings have re-spooked Scotty, who stares grimly ahead, and Lucky, who prods at my arm — 'Ka-ka-ka!' — from his perch on a little shelf next to the wheel. In the few minutes left before we reach the bar, I repeat last night's rationale: all we have to do is follow the GPS from one waypoint to the next. The first is already behind us; the second — to which we're now heading — is at the seaward end of the Washing Machine area, and the last is in safe water beyond the bar. By sticking to this proven course, we'll avoid the banks where swells can rear into breaking waves.

Real danger occurs only when the swell is much larger than today and breaks across the designated channels, or when — like *Shrieker* — a boat tries to cross where it shouldn't. (I do have one niggling concern: despite many costly repairs, our old Perkins diesel — dubbed

'Charlie' by an Aboriginal friend — remains unpredictable under pressure.)

But there's no time to go into that because we're suddenly in the grip of the Washing Machine. It's like a mechanical bull ride, with every part of the boat dipping and diving and bucking at once. Catapulted from his shelf, Lucky ascribes a spectacular arc right across the cabin. Scotty lets go of the upright she's clinging to and, like the netball whiz she used to be, plucks the flying terrier from the air before they sprawl cursing and snorting on the sofa.

Our speed is down to 3 knots against the tide and wind, but I'm not game to increase power in case Charlie Perkins overheats. We crawl on towards the second waypoint. On either side of us (sometimes only 50 metres away) swells roll onto sandbanks and explode into white water. Then the wind picks up, right on the nose, and I have to increase power or risk being pushed off course. By the time we pass the second waypoint and line up the final one, the temperature gauge is climbing and diesel smoke wafts through the cabin. (Fortunately, as a general rule, women and dogs rarely examine engine gauges.)

It takes a long time to reach the last waypoint. In the final stages we encounter a set of ever steeper three-metre swells, the last of which has our bow pointing at blue sky before Trady claws over the top and smacks down the other side. And that's it: we're through the bar! I throttle back a bit, turn off the wind so that the mainsail better assists our progress, and watch — chilled by drying sweat — as the temperature slips back to normal.

Scotty radios the coastguard to confirm our crossing and describe conditions. Within seconds another yacht calls us: 'Great to hear your voice, *Tradewind*,' says an American woman. 'That crazy guy who came in blind had us all worried. We're about to come out ourselves, so thanks for the report.'

An hour later, to much joyful shouting and barking, the wind gods kill off the opposing southerly and replace it with a nice little 10-knot nor'westerly, tailor-made for the run home.

EIGHT

Three dogs mosey through a dusty boatyard-cum-dry dock on the banks of a mangrove creek near Brisbane. Every few metres, they pause to piss in relays on a rusted engine block, or sniff at a sinister-looking puddle, or check out something intensely fishy amid the ruins of an old trawler. To a passer-by, the dogs might seem like old friends. In fact, from the moment they met, two of them have been an epic boatyard dogfight waiting to happen.

It's our first week at the yard, where Trady is up on blocks awaiting a new diesel and a complete repaint, major surgery that will keep her out of the water at least a month. We've taken leave for the project, and hired Nick to help during his university semester break. He doesn't arrive until a few days after us, when Lucky — still Jake's devoted follower — is overjoyed to see his idol spring from the familiar ute. Waggling and snorting, he leads Jake on a tour of the yard.

From our elevated position on deck, we watch Lucky introduce Jake to his new friend, Grunter. 'Uh-oh,' says Nick, as the two begin their sniffing manoeuvres, 'that's the sort of dog Jake always has trouble with.' Grunter is the ultimate alpha mongrel: barrel chest, massive jaws, dull eyes and scars everywhere. He's the same height as Jake, but wider and heavier, with the stolid, pushy air of a small-town policeman. Which, in a way, he is: owned by the slipway manager, Grunter is the yard's after-hours watchdog, spending his nights chained to a steel stake near the office.

Each morning when they meet, Lucky rolls into the submissive position and lets Grunter work him over with his battered nose. But this doesn't happen with Jake. And after a few days of such insubordination, Grunter makes a stand. Next time they meet, the yard cop shoves past Jake and pisses like a small horse before raking the ground with such force, rocks fly across the yard and bounce off a parked car. Jake circles a few times, then squirts into the same puddle left by Grunter: a direct challenge. Lucky moves off a little and crouches in the shade, glancing nervously up at us.

'Grrrrr!' says Grunter, hackles up.

'Grrrrr!' says Jake, kicking up a rock storm of his own.

'Jake! No!' Nick jumps down and hauls his dog away.

For the rest of the day, while Lucky, Grunter and other mutts continue their rounds of the yard, Jake is confined to the deck of the boat.

Next morning, while Nick and I are crammed into the engine well, struggling to free the old diesel from its rusted mounts, the inevitable brawl breaks out on the ground below. By the time we get there, two workmen have Grunter and Jake by the hind legs and are trying to drag them apart.

But the dogs keep breaking free and hurling themselves at one another's throats. There are bloodcurdling snarls, screams of pain, outraged shouts ('Hang on! ... Get the fuckin' hose! ...

Kick its arse!'), and a mad, dusty blur of flying stones, upset paint cans, tangled electrical leads and sprawling, cursing men. Despite his athleticism, Jake is no match for Grunter's terrible vice-like jaws, which lock on an upper leg and can't be dislodged.

Over a few dream-like seconds, when Jake's screams seem to go on and on, I see my son shove a workman aside, grab Grunter by the scruff of the neck and deliver two quick punches to the side of his head. The mighty watchdog goes limp.

Nick scoops up Jake and stumbles down the boatramp into the creek ... to bathe his wounds, he explains later. 'I had no idea I was going to do any of that,' he tells us, still wide-eyed. 'I just saw all that blood, and I thought, "I have to wash Jake now, or he'll die". It was the only thing in my head.'

Of course, Jake doesn't die, suffering only a few puncture wounds and a brief bout of humility. After a few moments repose, Grunter stirs himself and totters off to his favourite chemical puddle for a reviving drink. The slipway manager thinks it's a huge joke, and within a couple of days Jake and Grunter are shaping up for round two. Then something amazing happens, showing that even after two years our mystery terrier still has his secrets.

Lucky and Jake are on the ground near the two-metre-high stepladder at Trady's stern when Grunter and another tough yard dog spot them and close in. I'm about to climb down or throw something when Lucky hops onto the ladder and ascends briskly to the deck. Then he barks down at Jake, who sits looking up and whining. When Grunter and his mate are almost to him, Jake starts climbing the ladder. Not quite believing my eyes (as with the cushion incident at sea) I call Scotty.

Jake freezes halfway up, his long legs in a tangle, and has to be helped to the top. Once he's there, Lucky darts to the edge and startles Grunter with a volley of taunting barks. When the yard dogs have left, I take our little genius to the ground and get Scotty to call him from the deck. He trots straight back up the ladder. Within a few days, Jake has mastered it too, although neither can descend. From then on, when we hear them clattering up the ladder it usually means Grunter is paying a visit.

A rule of thumb: spend every spare cent you have on a boat, and it will remain in roughly the same condition; stop spending, and it'll deteriorate fast.

Another rule: impractical people (like journalists) who own boats hold no cards in their dealings with tradesmen. They can feign knowledge and try to bluff through, or front as confessed innocents with the capacity to pay. The first option doesn't work — 'Is it a centrifugal impeller driven by a V-belt from the crankshaft?' the diesel mechanic will ask — and the second almost guarantees they'll pay a hefty, gouge-the-sucker surcharge.

As the days pass at the boatyard, we fill a fruit carton with receipts for paint, sandpaper, filler, disposable overalls, dust masks, stainless-steel screws and bolts, hire tools, marine ply, fibreglass resin, etc. And then there's the big items: a new 60-horsepower diesel and the conversion of the existing gearbox, a new shaft and propeller, replacement wiring, new batteries. Last, but in no way least, is the cost of the mechanic to fit the new diesel, the painters to spray Trady's exterior after we've sanded and prepared it, and the weekly rent at the yard.

What sustains us through all this sweaty labour and money haemorrhaging is, of course, the Cruising Dream. In a few years, we remind each other, Trady will be both our home and our ticket to paradise. And not just for six months like last time, but for years.

'We'll roast fish in our new rotisserie oven,' calls Scotty from some sweltering hole where she's toiling with a sanding block.

'And serve them on deck in banana leaves with a garnish of rock oysters,' I cry, though sickened by the odour of the yard's notorious septic tank.

'We'll never have a schedule,' she shouts, 'except to check out every island, cay, reef, headland and bay along the way.'

'We'll never interview another mindless fucking celebrity!' I scream, nursing a just-skinned knuckle. 'Except for that famous tribe in New Caledonia that worships Prince Philip and carved him a massive codpiece.'

One morning, about halfway through Trady's makeover, there's a knock on the hull near the stepladder. It's a sandy-haired boy we've seen around the yard, and wriggling in his arms is Lucky. 'Would this be your little dog?' he asks.

I tell him it would, and his face falls.

'That's too bad,' he says. 'Because this is *exactly* the sort of dog I've been looking for, and there aren't many around.'

Where has he been looking?

'Oh, all around,' he says. 'I'm always on the lookout. But most stray dogs are quite big, and Dad says it has to be a little one.' He tries to press his face against the still-struggling Lucky, who growls his frustration.

'Better put him down,' coaxes Leisa. 'He's not much of a cuddler, anyway.'

Once free, Lucky bolts up the ladder.

'Wow,' says the boy. 'That's definitely the sort of dog I need.'

From then on Sam turns up regularly to play with Lucky and help with the interminable sanding. For the past five years (roughly half his life) he's lived with his father on a small yacht moored just off the slipway. Tall and blue-eyed, Sam appears to have time-travelled from an era predating the unholy mating of children and fashion. He wears faded shorts and T-shirts without advertising, his feet are broad and tough-soled, and his limbs show the scars of ambushes by oyster beds and rusty stakes and other cruel things that wait in creeks. (Seeing him cross the yard whistling to himself, or setting off in a dinghy to fish for bream, brings an odd sense of watching myself a long time ago.)

The most compelling thing about Sam is his enthusiasm. 'This fish burger,' he declares one lunchtime, 'is the best thing I've eaten since probably 1997.' He closes his eyes and chews the last bit. 'Mmm,' he says. 'I don't think there's anything better than fish!' In payment for his help, we give Sam bits and pieces he can use in the restoration of his own little sailboat. And fish burgers from a nearby takeaway.

Sam knows everyone around the boatyard and brings us up to date on their domestic arrangements. 'That's Sally,' he says, when a powerful-looking woman in brief denim shorts crosses the yard dragging a dainty suitcase on wheels. 'She used to live with Merv. But he drank and drank, so she's moving in with Russ.' An ancient, elongated mongrel inches by on tiny legs. 'Hiya, Centipede!' calls Sam, and the animal pauses, wagging its hairless tail. 'That's the oldest dog on this river,' the boy reports. 'Much, much older than me.'

Sam tells us his mother had been ill for most of her life, and almost died during his birth. After his parents parted, he came to live with his father because she was too sick to care for him. His father does odd jobs around the boatyard and at other marginal enterprises along the creek's muddy banks. When he isn't at school or helping us, Sam earns a bit more by removing foul-smelling muck from the bilges of several battered trawlers moored nearby.

The old drunk who looks after the trawlers tells me the boy is a hard worker but 'fulla shit', and that kids should be seen and not heard.

This view seems pretty general around the yard. 'Most people say, "Shut up, Sam,"' the boy tells us cheerfully. 'I can say gidday and stuff, then I have to be quiet. I have think-talks sometimes, but then I forget I'm only thinking the talk and say the words, and people go, "Hey, is Sam drunk, or what?"'

Some things the boy tells us reflect the hours he spends listening to lonely men (females are 'trouble' and drinking rum makes even good mates fight), and some, like his accounts of far-flung sailing adventures with his dad, a one-time 'Olympic sailing champion', probably stem from the chats he usually has with himself. Over a month, we don't see him with another kid.

Bored with the boat work, Lucky starts trailing Sam about the yard.

Sometimes, with our permission, the boy takes him further along the creek to fish from a rock wall, or to visit his 'best friend': a Vietnamese woman who lives in a neighbouring caravan park with her elderly husband. 'She talks more than me,' Sam says. 'When I go there, she always says, "Sammy! What's the news?" And before I can talk, she tells me all her news ...'

Beyond the waterfront, where the quick turnaround vessels are positioned, the boatyard broadens to accommodate a number of high-and-dry yachts, launches and homemade oddities. Here, another of Sam's hangouts, long-term residents have created gardens and picnic areas amid rusting machinery and abandoned hulks. Known as Sprouts (for taking root), some have lived this way for years, popping in and out of their decomposing boats like crabs whose greater purpose is understood only through patient observation.

Some have abandoned hope of returning to the water; some have never really been there (despite years of 'readying' their self-built craft), and some, like 'Polyp', have scared themselves ashore. A long time ago, according to yard gossip, Polyp almost drowned when his small sloop was rolled by a wave during a bar crossing. The damage wasn't extensive, but Polyp decided to reinforce the hull before returning to sea. He toiled for a year in cramped, airless places, fitting extra ribs and bedding them in great mounds of glass resin. He strengthened the bow, rebuilt the transom, added weight to the keel. Then he fitted heavier rigging, bigger winches, thicker anchor chain.

When finally refloated, Polyp's once spritely yacht was so burdened it almost sank on the spot. It was returned to the yard, where poor Polyp spent more years trying to reverse what he'd done. In the process, he spouted dozens of wart-like nodules around the eyes and mouth, which gave rise to his nickname and the theory that he was a victim of fibreglass poisoning. He became a serious drinker, falling so far behind in the struggle against rot and rust that his boat was effectively buggered. But he never acknowledged this, and nobody at the yard laboured the point.

Now Polyp and his drinking mate do regular social tours of the yard, pausing often to give the 'rush-rush crowd' (meaning anyone on a schedule) the benefit of their experience. If a newcomer mentions the name of any local tradesman whose services he plans to use, Polyp groans ominously while rubbing his thumb and forefinger together. 'Got shares in Microsoft, have ya?' chimes his mate, on cue. Sniggering contentedly, they roll on.

The oddest Sprout, by a long shot, is known as Captain Barrel. Named for his ridiculous boat — a series of plastic drums lashed together atop a rusty pontoon — he's a secretive, ill-tempered man who rides a noisy old motorbike and is rumoured to have done time for violent crimes. Captain Barrel is Sam's bogeyman.

'If you see him coming, watch out for Lucky,' the boy warns. 'He hates a lot of things, but mostly he hates dogs.'

Like most of Sam's information, this turns out to be spot-on.

According to other yard denizens, Barrel is a serial intriguer whose malicious gossip has left him friendless. He's also a rule freak who wants dogs banned from the yard (for chasing his motorbike), and a part-time evangelist who hangs about on street corners threatening sinners with eternal damnation. For us, the worrying thing is that Lucky hates motorbikes almost as much as Barrel apparently hates dogs.

(He's been that way since we got him. Once, when a dozen outlaw bikies left a Bundaberg café and fired up their hogs at the kerb, Lucky slipped his collar and tore around and around them barking maniacally. No one could catch him until the laughing desperados agreed to stop their motors, when he immediately lost interest.)

Since then, unaccountably, he ignores large motorbikes and only goes after farty little two-stroke jobs, which have the same despised pip-pip note as lawn trimmers and mowers. Unfortunately, Captain Barrel's ancient two-stroke is particularly farty, and one afternoon

— only a few days before we leave the yard —
the evangelist and the short-arsed terrier reach
their inevitable denouement. The incident itself
isn't much: Barrel pips by, and for the first time
Lucky rushes after him barking. Barrel stops
and tries to kick him. Then he gets off the bike,
takes a length of wood from the saddlebag and
strides towards us.

While Scotty grabs Lucky and puts him in the
car, I step forward and try to apologise. Barrel
keeps coming until we're almost touching. He
looks about 50, with pale eyes and bad teeth.

'I could kill that dog,' he says in a doom-
laden tone, pointing his stick towards Lucky.
'If not today, then tomorrow, and if not
tomorrow, then ...'

The smell of him is sickly sweet, with putrid
undertones, like wood rot in a confined space.

'No need for threats,' I tell him. 'He's just a
little dog. I'm sorry he ran out at you, but if you
got that muffler fixed maybe dogs wouldn't—'

'I've done it before,' he cuts in, still watching
Lucky. He waves his stick towards the creek.
'Dirty, stinking dogs should be tied up. Dirty,
stinking dogs that aren't tied up can go in the
creek. Eh? Eh?'

Around this point I decide to play it his way: mad and bad. 'Fuck off, you twisted little bastard!' (He steps back, and for the first time looks directly at me.) 'I know where you live,' I snarl. 'And if anything happens to Lucky, I'll come around and ram your stupid fucking boat up your arse, barrel by barrel.'

He takes another step back. 'I'm reporting you,' he says primly, and turns on his heel. That's when we see Grunter sauntering across the yard towards the motorbike, still spluttering on its stand. 'Get away!' screams Barrel. But it's too late: hoisting a leg, Grunter gives the troublesome machine a Niagara-like dousing. Even after Barrel hurls his stick, Grunter continues sploshing his bright yellow waste all over the bike's dusty paintwork.

'God, that was good,' laughs Scotty on the way home. 'I've never seen a dog produce so much piss! And the way the slipway manager just giggled while Barrel was raving. I think he was smoking a joint when Barrel burst into his shed.'

Our final days at the yard involve the usual whirl of last-minute jobs. Sensing the urgency, Polyp and his drinking mate drop by more often. 'Rush, rush, rush,' says Polyp. 'Go, go, go.'

On the last morning — with our launch due on the afternoon tide — Sam stops by and offers to take Lucky fishing while we put the final touches to our gleaming craft.

'I'm probably going to miss you a fair bit,' he says, staring into Lucky's face. 'Apart from my uncle's dog, who is smart but very old, I've never met a dog quite like you.'

'Kaark!' says Lucky, gazing back at him.

We watch them head off along the creek bank; Lucky pausing to check out rat smells among the rocks, then bounding on in response to Sam's calls. Hours later, when we finally leave, the boy climbs a high post next to the slipway and waves dramatically. 'Bye Lucky!' he cries. 'I hope you live a long, long time!'

The last we see of the boatyard before rounding a bend in the creek is a forest of stationary mast tops, their little wind vanes pointing hopefully seaward.

NINE

It's a bright spring morning at our new home by the sea. When I open my eyes, the first thing I see is Lucky standing on the bed watching me. He looks eager but impatient, as though he's been waiting for some time. The instant he realises I'm awake his mouth pops open, his ears and eyebrows change position, his eyes gleam and his whole face lights up.

'Kaark!' he snorts, and belly-crawls over to execute his now standard single nose lick. When I ruffle his ears he buzzes a little, rolls over against my shoulder and presses his silken head into my neck. Pretty soon (knowing it'll be at least an hour before Scotty stirs), he's sound asleep. I wouldn't mind reading, but reaching for the book might disrupt things so I resist the impulse. Through the window, I watch a lone white yacht slicing across Moreton Bay.

Our roomy, glass-fronted rental house is right on the waterfront at Woody Point, 30 minutes north of Brisbane on the Redcliffe Peninsula. In the city, it would have brought double the rent, but sleepy old 'Reddy' has yet to be discovered by the gentrification armies whose burgeoning numbers ultimately drove us from Bulimba. Another advantage is that we're now just ten minutes from the marina where the newly resplendent Trady is berthed, awaiting the sort of finishing touches we can apply on weekends.

Months have passed since the clash with Captain Barrel at the boatyard, yet it's still in my thoughts. *Dirty, stinking dogs should be tied up ... Dirty, stinking dogs can go in the creek ... I've done it before*. It was the vehemence that lingered, the absolute conviction behind his loathing. (In a dream not long after it happened, I saw Barrel in one of those End Is Nigh sandwich boards, hissing at strangers to repent. Next morning, I told Scotty: 'Sam and I have the same bogeyman.')

Was it just coincidence that this obviously damaged man is also some sort of religious fundamentalist? Probably. Yet in scientifically enlightened times it's hard to see a distinction between a literal acceptance of, say, Genesis (God created man in order to give him dominion over all other species that lack 'souls') and other common forms of madness.

Stretching out an arm, I manage to grab the animal psychology book I've been reading without disturbing the sleepers. (Since Lucky entered the scene, I've become addicted to the genre and can't pass a bookstore without picking up the latest offering.)

Towards the end of *Dogs Never Lie About Love*, author/psychoanalyst Jeffrey Moussaieff Masson suggests the Judeo–Christian take on dogs, and animals generally, is at last losing ground to a more considered perspective: 'Slowly, very slowly, our world is beginning to understand, perhaps for the first time in history, that humans are not the apex ... of creation, but only part of a larger world. This means we must share our planet with many other creatures ... who have as much right to its bounty and purity as we.'

Like the dog-loving Masson, I'm not a religious man. Yet even in modern, secular societies, religious conditioning still has a remarkable impact on the way people treat dogs. And not just among obvious dingbats like Barrel. Until quite recently, most psychologists, philosophers, ethologists and scientists collectively opposed notions of animals having emotions, knowing compassion and feeling pain.

Small wonder that a lot of otherwise reasonable people still regard dogs as chattels with strictly physical requirements — alive, in some basic and amusing way, yet with none of the needs or complexities of sentient beings like themselves. Not long ago, some neighbours of ours took their child off for a week's holiday but left the family dog, old and blind, blundering about alone in their backyard. It had shelter and food, but howled piteously with loneliness and (one imagines) a growing fear that this sudden and terrible isolation might be permanent.

After a few days, I took over an old radio and set it playing near the dog's sleeping area, which seemed to help. The returning owners were amazed to hear of their pet's sustained grief — hardly less surprised, it seemed, than if I'd told them their wheelbarrow and lawnmower had wept inconsolably in their absence. Yet this otherwise considerate couple weren't at all contrite about the dog's suffering, just embarrassed by the inconvenience to their neighbours.

It's a mindset that suggests little curiosity over what Jeffrey Masson calls the 'unyielding mystery' at the heart of a dog: 'Just when we think we know them completely, we look into the eyes of a family dog and something about their radiance, their depth, gives us pause. "Who are you, really?" we are inclined to ask at that moment. The dog might smile, a familiar smile, but will not answer. They keep their deepest mysteries to themselves.'

There's no mystery about what most confined suburban dogs enjoy most: their daily walk — or 'exercise', as those of the disciplinarian school tend to call it. But anyone who gets closer to a dog soon learns that exercise is a secondary aspect of the ritual. It's a social thing: the captive pets' only chance to make contact with other dogs and take part in the complex rounds of pissing and sniffing that connect and sustain them. Within reason, this means walking at their pace and allowing them time to indulge in the unfathomable (to us) world of smells that engages dogs so deeply.

Disciplinarians see this as weakness. 'Who's walking who?' they quip, surging past at a pace more suited to masters of the universe. With their ever-ready choke chains, they become expert at preventing the dog they're dragging around the block from experiencing any hint of pleasure or sociability. Invariably, the walk is part of their own exercise regime, and they'll be damned if they're going to let some sniffy, pissy mutt mess with their cardiac conditioning.

At Woody Point, walks along the foreshore are a lot more relaxed. Old blokes stand yarning under shady trees while their dogs tear about the beach or paddle languorously in the shallows. There's a defiant, Cannery Row feel to the place evocative of its tight-knit, battler origins. (Each time the local council erects a sign banning dogs from the beach, someone knocks it down.) Being mostly elderly, the regular dog walkers have no schedule and amble along at a pace perfectly suited to their pets.

Even better, from Lucky's perspective, their dogs are mainly the small, sociable variety he likes. Within a few weeks, he has more mates to greet on his walks than he met in our entire year in Bulimba. There's Ralph the miniature foxy; Shaggy the deaf bitsa; Rosie the flirtatious fluff ball; George the ancient mongrel; and a trio of eternally urinating Chihuahuas known as The Pee Amigos. Lucky's best friend is Tim the terrier, whose owner — charmed by the depth of their attraction — lets Tim off the leash whenever we approach so the two of them can rush together in a flurry of flopping ears and waggling tails.

Lucky also befriends a spritely bum who lives out of a supermarket trolley and displays no hint of the social cringe expected of city-based deros. Whenever he passes our gate, the whiskered, gravel-voiced drinker pauses to chat to Lucky, who responds with the buzzing and air-pawing he reserves for a favoured few. 'Is that *right*?' the bum might exclaim, grinning at him. 'Well, little buddy, I wouldn't have believed it if it hadn't come from a reliable source like your good self!'

The drifter has a similar effect on people. While parked near an intersection in the local shopping centre, we see him stop his trolley alongside an old man with a walking frame who's waiting to cross the street. 'Race you across!' the bum cries, and to the delight of onlookers they go for it — laughing and jostling like teenagers before reaching the opposite kerb neck-and-neck and pausing to shake hands.

But not everyone in our new neighbourhood gives an impression of having just ambled from a Steinbeck yarn. There's also a small but vocal element who might have goose-stepped directly from *Mein Kampf*.

Mostly men over 50, they're bias repositories of the type first drawn forth by that prejudicial divining rod, Pauline Hanson. Now they've become triumphant champions of Hanson's 'ideas' as repackaged by the Howard Government.

A handful of them have been blitzing local newspapers with letters tearing into anyone critical of Howard's stealthy commitment to the Iraq debacle — the details of which, one such writer indignantly asserts '... we have no need to know'. (Even in my father's era, such malleable souls — often Dad's biggest supporters — tended to live in country areas or regional centres like Redcliffe, attracting the tag 'rural idiot fringe'.)

One ruddy-faced ex-military man is known for dragging his ageing beagle on brutal daily route marches along the foreshore.

'See them big turds scattered along the path there?' drawls one of the more laidback dog walkers. 'That's because he won't even let his poor bloody dog stop for a crap.'

Only a few days later we see this act of torture occurring just ahead of us: as the beagle tries to crouch, its owner shouts 'Oi!' and yanks it off balance, then forges on with the animal stumbling helplessly in his wake.

A week after that, while exploring new parts of the suburb, we see The Dragger reclining in the open front room of his home, a large poster of Pauline Hanson with the legend 'I Told You She was Right!' displayed on the wall behind him.

It's around this time that Lucky develops a fascination with the lorikeets that zoom among the waterfront banksias. One morning, while he's examining a tree for parrot activity, The Dragger powers past us with his traumatised pet.

Lucky is okay with the leash by this stage, but unless we're among traffic he walks by himself — and to hell with the by-laws. Spotting the beagle, he trots over, waggling engagingly, to make its acquaintance.

'Oi!' growls The Dragger, and wrenches his poor beast away. After a few steps he stops and glares back at Lucky, who has resumed his position under the tree, head cocked, listening for the oddly amplified lorikeet chatter he finds so intriguing. The Dragger shakes his head with the pained satisfaction of the truly embittered.

'Doin' what he wants,' he says disgustedly. 'Doin' exactly what he bloody well wants.' As though that was the last thing on earth a man should allow a dog to do.

TEN

Each morning after Leisa leaves for work in the city, Lucky climbs onto a cushion beneath my desk for a snooze. I rarely see him leave, yet the next time I look he's usually in the pile of clean laundry that we — indifferent homemakers — dump on a bed in the adjacent spare room. From my desk, I can see through the doorway the tip of his curly noggin poking from the tangled mass of towels, sheets and undies.

'Hey Luckster,' I call, partly to waste time but also because I love the way his head pops up with eyes owlishly wide and floppy ears askew.

'Kaark!' he says. We stare at each other for a while before his eyelids droop and he sinks helplessly back into his nest.

Doin' what he wants, I tell myself. It's now almost four years since Lucky rode Scotty's shoulders home from Death Row, and The Dragger's lament has become our way of acknowledging his finest moments. Because doing what he wants (meaning, of course, the trust-and-friendship approach) seems to have settled most of Lucky's hang-ups and made him an ever more engaging little mate.

People we've just met tell us he's the happiest dog they've encountered, and friends are intrigued by the way he formally seeks to convey his appreciation for this state of affairs. Each morning, for example, after we get home from his beloved walk, Lucky approaches Scotty and me separately with much waggling and snorting to thank us for the outing. Only then does he curl up for a pre-breakfast nap. (This routine began about a year ago and doesn't vary.)

At other times, if one of us seems a bit down in the dumps, he'll study them a while then race across the room, seize one of his stuffed animals, and with a flick of the head, spin it through the air to land on or near the gloomy one. Then he'll move in with his air pawing, mini-stallion routine, as if to say: 'C'mon, snap out of it!'

He hates any hint of conflict, even mildly raised voices. If we argue, his ears and tail droop and his expression becomes woebegone. He moves close and looks imploringly from me to Scotty, never whining but touching our legs with a paw until it's impossible to ignore him. 'Pfft!' he says. ('No!') 'Pfft! Pfft!'

'Okay, okay,' one of us will relent, and scoop him up for a three-way hug. (As soon as friendly relations are restored, he goes off about his business.)

Now about six and approaching middle-age, Lucky has long since stopped doing runners in parks and seems to have accepted his arrangement with us as permanent. Not surprising, really: he has a choice of beds and sofas, never spends more than a few hours alone, tags along on all holidays and has yet to set foot in a boarding kennel. Thanks to the travel-bag system, he even scored two illicit nights in a luxurious high-rise apartment on the Gold Coast. (The jig seemed to be up when Lucky's head popped from the bag and startled a lift full of Chinese tourists only minutes after check-in. 'Guide dog,' Scotty ad-libbed, pointing at the grinning head. 'Very portable!' The Chinese frowned and looked thoughtful, but didn't dob us in.)

Over the years, Lucky has dined at dozens of sidewalk cafés. He takes great pleasure in being served his own bowl of water, and always makes a show of drinking as soon as it arrives because it pleases the waiters. 'Aren't you a thirsty little boy!' they exclaim, crouching to pat him. 'Kaark!' he says, gazing soulfully into their faces. After which nothing is too much trouble.

In our experience, inner-city Sydney cafés are a lot more dog friendly than their Brisbane counterparts, perhaps because of the self-consciousness implicit in the smaller city's relentless quest to 'come of age'.

'No dogs, no horses, no pigs,' snapped a sallow waif at a Bulimba café where we once sought a meal. In contrast, the bulky Italian owner of an eatery in Sydney's Leichhardt took such a shine to Lucky he kept diving under our table to feed him ethnic titbits: 'Hey, Mr Lucky, try this one! My own mother's secret recipe! You like?'

But for the most entertaining dining-with-dog experiences, it's hard to go past our own Redcliffe. Still a bit new to the outdoor dining scene, its first wave of waterfront cafés vie for space with the pawn shops and bargain warehouses that have dominated the retail strip for decades. Lucky's favourite breakfast joint is near a pharmacy offering a huge array of rental wheelchairs, prostheses and walking aids. One morning, as we plough through a couple of Hangover Specials on the pavement, Lucky hurtles from beneath the table and tries to attack a motorised wheelchair ridden by an old man in a cowboy hat.

The leash pulls him up short, but there's a collective gasp of horror and outrage from a group of tourists at the next table. I see Cowboy Hat with his merry drinker's face taking all this in before he assumes a terrified expression and waves his arms in the air. 'Me legs, me legs!' he screams. 'He's after me legs!' By now several of the tourists are braced for action, and we're all staring at the old bloke's imperilled legs. Except there are no legs, just a pair of empty pants flapping in the breeze.

'Har, har, har!' roars Cowboy Hat. 'Got yiz with that one! I haven't had legs for yonks.' He trundles closer to Lucky and scratches his ears. 'But if you'd like a coupla nice meaty knee bones,' he says, 'they've probably still got me old ones up at the hospital. They'd be a bit ripe by now, I reckon, but that wouldn't worry a wild beast like you, eh mate!' The tourists hurriedly turn their chairs away, but Lucky makes such a fuss of the old larrikin he lingers right through breakfast, bawling out details of ever more grisly medical problems.

On another occasion Scotty and I are relaxing outside a hotel at Woody Point when a patron calling himself a 'retired Sydney hit man' sprawls out of the public bar, collapses near our table and tries to kiss Lucky on the lips.

'I *love* dogs,' he tells us with tears on his cheeks. 'Nobody could pay me enough to kill a dog. But people? Well, there were times when I did it for free.'

One thing leads to another until, against the advice of bar staff, we invite him home for a drink. About 60, he uses the confronting alias Dirk Ponsonby, and entertains us for hours with dark tales from his past and imitations of the moist, gurgling noises people make after being shot in the stomach at close range.

Things get a bit tricky later when Dirk starts chasing Scotty around the lounge, but he's only a little ex-killer so Lucky and I herd him outside and bid him a firm farewell. He assures me there are no hard feelings, and that under no circumstances would he ever try to gut-shoot such a convivial couple, '... especially Leisa'.

In spite of all this socialisation the short-arsed terrier remains, deep down, a wild little bastard who can morph in an instant from 'cute puppy' (his favoured disguise among children and old folk) to crazed marauder. There are various triggers for this, but cats still top the list. One of our neighbours has a beautiful collie-cross we call The Yodeller. Sweet natured and deeply sociable, she emerges each morning as we pass her open gate, and lifts her golden head and lets fly with a high, fluting yowl of greeting.

Yet Lucky knows — through long and malevolent observation from our gate — that

The Yodeller is actually an appalling traitor who shares her home with a *cat*. Even worse: she and the fat ginger feline play together on their front lawn, in full public view! So he evolves a plan: each morning when The Yodeller comes out to greet us and is distracted by our pats, he skips around her and scuttles unnoticed down her driveway, then roots out the cat and gives it a taste of old-fashioned dog terror.

Of course, after a few such successful raids, The Yodeller is on to him.

The moment he hits the driveway, she breaks away from us and — yodelling frantically — bustles after him. Amazingly, she tries to protect the cat by blocking Lucky's progress with her body and then using her lowered head in an effort to bulldoze him off the property. But once he realises she's too gentle to actually attack, Lucky eludes her easily and drives the enraged cat into the sort of tight spots where she can't follow. With cats, he remains an unreasoning brute: once on a chase, nothing — including our most forceful commands and even the hurling of shoes and umbrellas — will deter him.

A journalist friend who looks after Lucky at his home for a day experiences this first-hand.

When Adrian (who once battled Lucky for the sofa during our passage to Gladstone) takes his charge into the yard for a leak, they encounter Max the Manx, a one-eyed standover cat who terrorises local dogs. 'Max and Lucky saw each other simultaneously,' Adrian later reports in a note to us.

'Max went into his Cool Hand Luke stretching routine to show his contempt, but Lucky just ran straight at him, barking and growling hysterically. Midway through a really impressive back arch, Max suddenly saw the flaw in his strategy (he was dealing with a really *mad* dog), abandoned his pose and streaked over the fence.'

Motorbikes have slipped down Lucky's hate list, while mowers, lawn trimmers and chainsaws now generate almost as much loathing as cats. A recent addition to his MUST KILL category are the bulbous little puffer fish that hang about the pontoons at the marina where we keep Trady. Trotting behind us along these floating walkways, he scans constantly for the despised species while ignoring all others.

When he spots one he digs in against the leash and growls with such amplified fury that yachties pop wide-eyed from their cabins, fearing some sort of attack. It didn't take long for the live-aboard regulars to evolve their own name for him. 'It's okay, honey,' I hear an elderly American call below to his wife after one of Lucky's thunderous fish rages. 'It's only The Crazy Commodore.'

ELEVEN

It's been more than a year since Lucky saw Jake, yet his excitement when Nick's ute pulls up outside our house is as intense as ever. Yipping and leaping in the air, he greets his hero then belts joyously around the property for a while before noticing that Jake hasn't moved from a patch of lawn just inside the gate. From the veranda, we see Lucky bustle inside and return with a stuffed toy, which he lays at Jake's feet. No reaction. So he brings another, and another. But Jake just stands there in the blistering sun, staring fixedly at the ground.

Perplexed, Lucky makes another trip inside and emerges with his newest toy: a talking, khaki-clad Steve Irwin doll. 'Crikey! Crikey!' it yammers as he wrestles it down the steps and across the yard. 'Danger, danger!' When Jake still doesn't respond, Lucky sniffs at his drooping muzzle before slumping dejectedly in some nearby shade.

Nick coaxes Jake inside and gives him a drink, then flops down on a sofa and describes the biological horrors that reduced his once-proud companion to the quavering invalid before us.

It began months earlier in the tropical heat of Townsville, where Nick and another science student at James Cook University share a house near a tributary of the Ross River. Apart from mosquito-born diseases like Ross River virus, the marshy wastelands of South Townsville are notorious for ticks.

Jake spent his days alone at the property, which was fenced but not well enough to prevent him occasionally going AWOL. And despite two recent spray treatments, the rented house itself remained tick-infested; each afternoon after Jake welcomed the homecoming students, they'd remove up to 50 of the tiny bloodsuckers from his body. The other element guiding Jake to his fate were the gangs of semi-feral dogs that roam the area at night, rooting and brawling like out-of-control armies.

One night Nick was wrenched awake by an uproar in the living room and ran out to find two strange dogs attacking Jake. 'They were tearing him apart,' he tells us. 'They took off when I arrived, straight out the door we always leave open for Jake. When I turned on the light I couldn't believe what they'd done to him. It was like a war zone, with blood and bits of flesh splattered everywhere.'

Next morning a vet put scores of stitches into Jake's many jagged, bone-deep wounds, and dispensed strong antibiotics to counter inevitable infections. Nick thinks Jake had been pursuing a neighbour's in-season bitch when set upon by one of the dog gangs and chased home. 'If he hadn't been close by,' he reasons, 'he'd never have made it. They would have killed him in the street.' Nick took the day off classes to nurse his patient. But even as they sat together on the veranda that morning, Jake spotted the neighbour's 'slinky' little bitch and in a twinkling leapt the fence and was gone.

Nick searched for him for days. He put up reward posters, scoured creek banks and mangrove swamps and made regular calls to the council. On the fifth morning, when he'd given up hope, he rose to prepare for uni and found Jake stretched out in the back of his ute in the driveway. Sick and exhausted, his wounds badly infected, he was crawling with ticks and barely able to acknowledge Nick's welcome.

Yet within a fortnight Jake seemed pretty much back to normal. It took a couple of months for the real toll of his carousing to emerge. First came a strangely clumsy fall as he rushed down some steps. Then, during a walk on the beach, he was approached by two friendly mutts no bigger than Lucky and immediately rolled into the submissive position, eyes wide with fear.

Nick stretches and rubs his face, exhausted by the long drive from Townsville. 'After that,' he says, 'he started not to look like himself anymore. His eyes changed. That's the worst thing: you look into his face and think, "Where's he gone? Where's Jake?"'

The vet confirmed Nick's fears: it was a 'brain thing', probably some form of degenerative meningitis, caused either by ticks or mossies or the infected wounds. Not long before they came south for the summer break, Jake suffered several convulsive fits and now seems unable to make left-hand turns.

L ater, while Nick sleeps, we witness the moment when Lucky, too, seems to recognise that Jake is no longer who he used to be. Stirring from a long slumber, Jake shuffles across the lounge and pauses near Lucky's prone form, peering down as though at some dimly remembered thing.

'Perhaps it's coming back to him,' says Scotty. Like me, she's thinking of their early times together — all those busy days and sociable nights with Jake and Lucky always part of the gang.

Jake stands there a long time, staring down.

'Why were you such a bastard to Lucky?' Scotty asks him, after a while. 'Why did you take his stuffed zebra and humiliate him?'

'Because I *could*,' I respond on Jake's behalf, in a deep, devil-may-care tone. 'And because he's a jumped-up little pissant with open space where his nuts should be, that's why.'

Scotty: 'That's rich. Coming from a big stud who just screwed his own brains out in a swamp.'

Jake: 'Cool it, bitch. You play hard and then you die. Or you live forever drooling under some geek's chair. I made my choice.'

Lucky's warning growl cuts through our nonsense; then his teeth are bared and he's on his feet snarling and driving poor Jake (the *real* Jake) away from him. The attack ends as abruptly as it began, but from that moment until Jake leaves the following afternoon, Lucky won't have anything more to do with him. Through some law-of-the-jungle instinct he's understood that his one-time idol is damaged goods and ditched him on the spot.

Nick points out that most dogs Jake has contact with have reacted the same way. 'They suddenly detect something about him that isn't right,' he says. 'And the way they respond is like: "Get away from me!" It's as though they fear he's contagious. If they were wild dogs, I guess they'd kill him.'

A couple of weeks later, after further tests in Brisbane confirm damage to Jake's brain, Nick and he make the same grim trip to the family vet that I made with Badger years before.

TWELVE

My parents died years before I met Scotty. I've told her about my quirky childhood and Dad's political obsessions, and how — after my brother Rob and I fled to Australia — our parents and Rusty the dog wandered for years between remote beach cottages, rediscovering something they'd lost early in the marriage. But for some reason I'd all but forgotten their trip to Australia in the late sixties.

It's not until Scotty and I buy a cottage in neighbouring Margate, and are packing to leave the rented beach house, that an old photo turns up to revive these fractured memories. It shows my father waiting for a bus on the Gold

Coast. Next to him on the seat is a battered suitcase, and at his feet — attached to a length of rope — is Rusty.

'Finished!' calls Scotty from across the room, where she's taped shut the last packing case ready for the removalists in the morning. It's late at night, and Lucky is sprawled across the contents of the family memorabilia box I was sorting until the yellowed snapshot stole my attention. Scotty settles beside us.

'What've you found?'

I show her the picture; a notation on the back confirms it was taken at the end of our parents' strange journey to Australia in 1969.

'Why strange?' asks Scotty.

'Well, Dad was seventy-something, and as usual they had almost no money beyond their fares. And they brought Rusty with them.'

At the time, Rob and I were long-haired surf bums living in a cheap Melbourne flat. We drove an old van with flowers painted on the doors and worked in a fishfinger factory. Dad had some idea of producing a travel book about the Gold Coast, but first he and Mum had to work alongside us in the factory to get money for their trip north.

'That is pretty strange. What did they do at the factory?'

'We all sorted fishfingers on the quality control line. We had to wear white coats and little plastic shower-cap things. But Dad's eyesight was so bad he could barely see the fishfingers, let alone spot the dodgy ones. Then he started pushing his conspiracy theories to the other workers, so they sacked him.'

Scotty wants to know more, of course. *Why* had my parents come? How did we all get on? And why did they bring Rusty?

I try to remember. It began with one of our father's long, worried letters. He worried about us being 'adrift' in a dangerous world, and felt responsible because it was their small, unhappy world we'd run away from. He worried about us getting into crime, or being conscripted, or preyed upon, or crashing our car, or drowning in the surf. But the only thing worrying us was a chilling reference in his letter to us all 'pooling our resources' when they came for their proposed visit.

Dad was a generous man who expected the same of others, the flaw in the equation being that he was almost always broke. His real purpose in coming was us. He hoped Rob and I would get involved in his travel-book project, and that we'd all get back together as a happy family living on the 'glorious' Gold Coast. That's probably why he brought Rusty: he wanted to stay permanently, and for everything to be as it was in the early, carefree days of their marriage.

But it was too late for that. His almost non-stop conspiracy harangues — anti-Semitic at core, with countless offshoots involving the economics of 'false debt' — had made our father pretty much unbearable, even to us. Mum had tuned out long ago. 'Thank God,' she said when he was sacked from the fishfinger factory. 'Now I can relax.'

For some weeks, Dad and Rusty stayed at home in our tiny flat. Rusty, deeply bored, slept and farted while Dad sat at his trusty Olivetti cranking out letters to editors about conspiracies. We dutifully pooled our resources. Somehow, by a process I can't remember, I ended up on the Gold Coast with our parents while Rob stayed in Melbourne. Within a few weeks, Mum took off back to New Zealand; Dad followed soon afterwards, his book project abandoned.

Nothing had worked out the way he'd hoped, yet he was never one to show his disappointment. 'Help me prepare this walking stick,' he said the day before he left. He produced a tin of white paint and a brush, explaining that he'd booked on the bus to Sydney as 'blind man and seeing-eye dog'. Of course, the coach driver objected when they turned up (Rusty looked nothing like a guide dog), but Dad ranted and waved his stick and eventually prevailed.

At the time I thought it was hilarious. The fact that my ageing father *was* almost blind, and had just a few dollars to get himself and our cast-off pet to Sydney and on to a (pre-paid) flight to Auckland, did nothing to lessen my amusement. And now I recall something else: it was me who suggested the picture of him and Rusty at the bus stop, because I fancied myself as a writer and thought it would make a funny story. A few years later, I worked it into a piece for the now defunct *Nation Review*. To my delight, they rejected the photo in favour of a sketch of a ragged, air-humping mongrel by the then rising star, Michael Leunig.

I don't want to think too much about how the old man must have been feeling that day, but in the photo he's wearing his famous stoic smile. (The same unconvincing grimace appears on his bony face in snaps taken while he was recovering from shrapnel wounds in a field hospital in Egypt, more than 50 years earlier.)

But he sure did come to love that dog, I tell myself, filing the picture away. Scotty and Lucky have gone to bed, but I have one last group of photographs to sort through. They're in a decomposing envelope marked 'Cottages/ Picnics', and show our parents and Rusty at various seaside locations in the years following their trip to Australia. As pointless as it seemed at the time, that trip turned out to be some sort of catalyst for all three of them.

On their return to New Zealand, they sold the family home, packed Rusty into their old Zephyr and roamed from one picturesque beach cottage to the next. In the process, Dad somehow reined in his obsessions and he and Mum became friends again. In almost every photo (mostly time-release shots of them picnicking amid sand dunes, or fishing, or settling in to yet another sunny cottage) two things stand out: their contentment, and Rusty's new role at the centre of it.

It shows in their relaxed faces; in the way they're invariably smiling at the dog's antics, or resting a hand on him, or feeding him things. Rusty, too, appears strangely renewed. After all those years in the background, he grins crookedly back at his people, like a dog with something to live for.

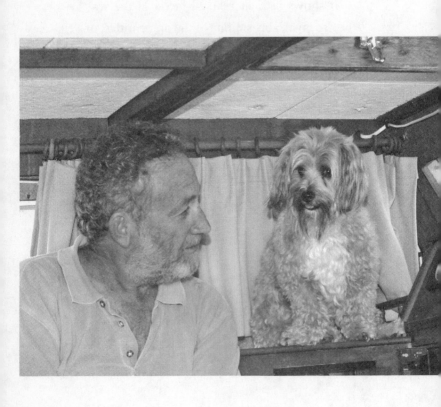

THIRTEEN

F rom the sea, the bay behind Double Island Point near Fraser Island appears to offer little real protection for boats. Even in moderate weather, the dominant southeast swell somehow curls around the protruding headland and makes comfort at anchor as unusual, according to one cruising guidebook, 'as integrity in politics'. So it seems on the morning when we round Double Island Point just before sunrise after a gentle night sail from Mooloolaba, 45 nautical miles to the south.

With Lucky tethered on deck and the powerful new diesel purring below, we make for a cluster of masthead lights (yachts at anchor) twinkling against a backdrop of towering sandhills at the bay's southern end. But it's soon obvious that the lights aren't so much twinkling as arcing wildly from side to side as the yachts roll in the small but pronounced swell. As we motor past them, our new digital depth sounder shows the yachts — all monohulls with deepish keels — are in 3–4 metres of water, as close as they can safely get to the beach.

We keep heading shoreward, as counselled by local fishermen, aiming for a saddle in the line of sandhills, their summits glowing in the first rays of sunlight. Now untied, Lucky trots to the tip of the bow and works the scented breeze with his nose, tail thumping the deck in anticipation. When the depth shows one metre, we turn left and run alongside the beach towards the bay's southern extremity.

All of a sudden the swell is gone — meaning we're behind a long sandbar that extends at right angles from the headland into the bay, forming a protected gutter of shallow water between itself and the beach. Little known except among locals, this is Double Island Point's unofficial 'lagoon' — typical of the many

Queensland coastal hideaways accessible only to shallow-draught vessels. We anchor with less than a metre below the keel, brew coffee and sit on the barely moving deck watching the bilious dance of the now-distant monohulls.

It's May 2006, and we've fled Brisbane for a few weeks to revive the Cruising Dream — so long anticipated, and so often delayed, it's starting to fray at the edges. The first proposed departure date, late 2004, flashed by with no hope of our finances being up to it. Our ETD then became early 2005; then late 2005; then early 2006 ... when we find we're *still* a year away from the Absolutely Final Time of Departure (AFTD), as we desperately know it.

It's depressing, especially when we read stories of other would-be cruisers who prepared so long and carefully for their great escape they eventually grew into people who didn't want to do it any more. On the other hand, we're determined to avoid tight schedules and cruise for several years, and unless you're independently wealthy (or happy to live like a bum), bailing out of society for that long requires commitment and a lot of organisation.

Addicts of the cruising life have inevitably likened it to sex: abstain long enough and the appeal fades. But take it up again and you wonder why you stopped. And while short jaunts about Moreton Bay are okay (in a coitus-interruptus sort of way), it wasn't until we left its confines and set sail up the coast for Double Island Point — with weeks of free time ahead — that the true pleasures of cruising came flooding back.

After a long, slow breakfast in our exclusive lagoon we go ashore to explore the headland. Lucky, too, seems revitalised by the setting: snoozing in suburban laundry piles isn't bad, but it doesn't rate alongside this magical bay with its squeaky white sand, fragrant shrubbery and — in shady groves at the foot of the sandhills — thrilling whiffs of dingo activity. In a whirr of flapping ears he races far ahead then hurtles back, swerving, barking, running mad circles and plunging about in water so clear it exposes in silvery detail a school of winter whiting streaking past just offshore.

At the tip of the headland we stop for a picnic and watch a pod of dolphins carving up the point break; miles to the north, across the glittering emptiness of Wide Bay, a red sail inches toward the bar entrance. Beyond that, the southern tip of Fraser Island peeks from beneath a wad of low cloud. We trek on through cypress pine, casuarina, banksia and patches of remnant rainforest, past the now automated lighthouse and down to the open surf beach.

Walking south towards the wreck of the *Cherry Venture* (a cargo ship bundled ashore by a cyclone in 1973), we can see the distant outlines of Noosa Heads and other Sunshine Coast landmarks passed during the sail up here last night. In holiday periods, this beach is dense with four-wheel-drive traffic. There isn't much today, but with an outgoing tide there are just enough vehicle tracks for my purpose — which is to introduce Scotty to one of the rare culinary happenings of my childhood: pipi fritters.

It took almost 200 years for white Australians to recognise these common surf beach shellfish as something other than bait. Yet even after European and Asian migrants put them on menus here — in pasta dishes, or steamed with rich XO sauces — the best way of preparing pipi, or eugarie, is still pretty much unknown outside New Zealand.

But first: the hunt. Even with Lucky's help, digging at random would be futile. Although just inches below the surface, mollusc beds move constantly and give no outward sign of their presence ... unless vehicles pass over them on hard sand, when little pressure mounds appear above each pipi. Using these telltales, the walk to the *Cherry Venture* and back yields enough good-sized specimens for dinner. Back on the boat, I put them unopened in a bucket of seawater, throw in a handful of flour (so they eject all sand and take in the flour), and leave them in a shady spot until later.

By late afternoon all the monohulls have left to cross the bar on the rising tide, leaving us alone in what we're starting to realise is one of the loveliest anchorages we've experienced. (On earlier overnight visits, before getting the low-down on the lagoon, we'd anchored only in the exposed outer bay.)

But we're not really alone: hearing a roar of outrage from Lucky, we hurry on deck in time to witness a sea eagle making off with part of his dinner. Rigid with fury, he watches the predator alight at its nest in a nearby dead tree. Moments later, it's hovering above us again, eyeing off the remaining portions of Lucky's chicken-wing meal.

Typically, he'd been atop the cabin in torpedo mode, contemplating his tucker, when the raider struck. (Unless another dog is present, when he gobbles everything immediately, Lucky's contemplation phase — a sort of gloating stocktake — can last up to ten minutes.) But now he prowls the deck growling up at this new threat to his cushy existence. When the eagle refuses to go away, he regales us with anxious snorts — 'Ka! Ka! Ka!' — as if to say, 'Do something!'

'Just bloody well eat it,' Scotty tells him. After another threatening swoop by the eagle, Lucky seizes the remaining chicken bits one by one and carries them into the cabin to complete the contemplation process under the table. Later, when a spectacular yellow moon has crested the headland, Scotty settles on deck with a bottle of white while I cook dinner.

Opened by hand and fed through an old steel mincer, the pipis make perfect fritters: light and crisp and bursting with the unique flavour that's never there when the shellfish are steamed or boiled open.

'Yeess!' cries Scotty, fork flying. 'Oh God, yes. Gimme more!'

We eat a dozen each, toss the remaining few to Lucky and go on deck to kill the last cold bottle.

The full moon is now directly overhead, illuminating the glassy lagoon so well we can discern every shell on the bottom and each passing fish as though through a magnifying glass. It's like floating in a giant martini. The silence seems absolute ... until we take turns closing our eyes and identifying sounds. There's the soft plop of feeding fish; the peculiar vibrating cry of the nesting sea eagle; tiny murmurings from countless birds concealed in the undergrowth; the occasional breathy gasp of a surfacing turtle, and — underlying all these — a muted grumble from the nearby surf beach.

As usual at such times, Lucky sits apart from us letting all this wash over his senses. His ears move constantly, and his swivelling nose plucks from the air scents so exotic he sometimes has to snort and shake himself before taking another sample.

As the days pass, we abandon plans to go further north and slip into the seductive rhythms of our little piece of paradise. The key to lazy cruising, we remind ourselves, is never to leave a place you're enjoying unless death or weather intervenes. (Using this principle, a couple we met on our 2000 cruise had been circumnavigating Australia in their old steel catamaran for 12 years.)

Each morning, we rise early and monitor weather reports, then take Lucky ashore for a long walk and a swim before breakfast. Then it's back to bed for a couple of hours reading and napping; then lunch and odd jobs about the boat followed by another shore expedition (snorkelling, fishing, exploring); then more reading/loafing until drinks around 5 pm, when we plan dinner and ready the beanbags for another bloody sunset.

The natural world has its own patterns, which soon become part of ours. At low water, hundreds of seabirds settle on the dry sandbank that shelters the lagoon; as the tide rises, they ascend in swarms to hunt fish until water covers the sandbank, when all species disappear almost simultaneously. 'The birds have gone,' one of us might call — meaning that for the next hour or so, until the tide drops and the sheltering sandbank reappears, we'll rock a bit more than usual.

A roar from Lucky on patrol means the thieving sea eagle is hovering, or a pod of dolphins is herding fish about the lagoon, or stingrays are lying on the bottom watching him with their big spooky eyes. With no TV, we sit on deck at night and watch our own sky channel, featuring non-stop weather action and live appearances by billions of refreshingly anonymous stars. On the eighth night, the stars vanish behind great wads of cloud and for the first time the wind swings north and blows directly into the bay.

At first light the next morning we're woken by wild rocking. It's almost low tide, yet wind-driven swells are surging over the exposed sandbank into the lagoon, reforming and breaking on the beach 50 metres behind us. Definitely time to go. But where? We study the cruising guides and Scotty votes for Noosa Heads: 'It's a downwind sail, and we can anchor for nothing in that little all-weather bay at the end of Hastings Street [Noosa's swanky restaurant/shopping strip].'

'Kaark!' snorts Lucky, who as usual is up on the table overseeing the decision making.

'Much eating and people-watching,' coaxes Scotty, warming to her wilderness-to-excess theme. 'And there's that great park for Lucky, right next to the anchorage. As long as he doesn't chase the scrub turkeys ...'

That afternoon a volunteer coastguard vessel leads us through the dangerous, shifting shoals of the Noosa bar and into the Noosa River. Just in time, too: nasty little squalls shot with lightning have shadowed us all the way from Double Island Point, and winds are predicted to reach gale force by nightfall.

With Lucky on lookout at the bow, we wind up the shallow river to a sheltered bay behind the man-made peninsula at the end of Hastings Street. This is where the bar used to be until decades ago, when the river mouth was moved a kilometre to the north to protect an expensive new canal estate from storm surges.

Back then, when Noosa was still a family resort, the bay we're in was part of a caravan park. Now it's the start of a long, wooded reserve whose maze of tracks are shared by joggers, dog walkers, and sunworshippers en route to secluded beaches near the revamped bar entrance.

We anchor with our stern only 20 metres from the sand; across the park, we can see Porsches and Ferraris doing circuits of Hastings Street. On the other side of the inlet, the dark-tinted windows of sprawling waterside mansions seem to stare reproachfully upon our proximity.

'Wow,' says Scotty, looking around. 'Talk about gypsies in the palace. If I'd paid millions for one of those big boxes, it'd really piss me off to have me anchoring out front for free.'

I notice a man in the park waving in our direction; at the same moment, my mobile phone — silent for over a week — starts ringing. It's our old friend and sailing companion, Des. 'I thought it must be you,' he says, still waving. 'We're having a picnic. There's plenty of champers and deli goodies if you'd like to join us. Lucky, too, of course.'

A few minutes later, still in grubby shorts and T-shirts, we join the picnickers on their white rug in the middle of the lush green park. Wearing a rakish fedora, Des — a Gatsby-like devotee of the good life — introduces us to his similarly elegant friends, breaks out more champagne flutes, and with a courtly gesture presents a bowl of chilled water to Lucky: 'There you go, me old shipmate.'

'Kaark!' says Lucky, who loves Des and hasn't stopped waggling since spotting him across the park. As he buries his nose in the bowl, a scrub turkey wearing what Des later identifies as a 'smug' expression trots past the picnic setting. 'Rrrrooor!' goes Lucky, upsetting his bowl. Ripping the leash from Scotty's fingers, he charges across the picnic rug — sending glasses and food flying — and hurtles after the fleeing turkey.

Those birds can really move: at top speed, like the road runner of cartoon fame, their legs revolve so quickly they appear to be on wheels. Yet Lucky stays right on its tail, impervious to our shouts and the horrified cries of other picnickers.

'Look out!' hollers a teenage boy. 'It's a giant ferret!'

'Get him! Get him!' yells a fat man in braces, making a lunge at Lucky and tripping over his own hamper.

The turkey throws some radical turns, which gain it a few metres but loses ground on the straights.

Round and round the park they go … until the loop on Lucky's leash snags on a bush, flipping him spectacularly onto his back, and the turkey escapes into a thicket. Frozen like figures in a Renoir scene, the picnickers stare at the panting, wild-eyed culprit.

'What a naughty, naughty little dog!' scolds an elderly woman, and with that they all sit down and resume their nibbling.

'Same old Lucky,' laughs Des, refilling the water bowl. 'Beautiful one moment, homicidal the next.'

The next day is cold and windy, so we dig out Lucky's jaunty red sailing jacket and zip him into it before heading ashore to do our laundry and reprovision the galley. Sunbleached and shaggy, with a piece of rope as a leash (the real one went missing in the park), he surges ahead of us up Hastings Street, looking very much the dashing seafarer out for a bit of sport ashore. We stop for lunch at a dog-friendly outdoor café, where the food is so good we book a table for an indulgent Noosa dinner that night.

Heading back to the boat, Scotty succumbs to a rare bout of window-shopping while Lucky and I sit nearby guarding the groceries. Suddenly, we're assailed by exotic perfume.

'Omigod!' squeals a young blonde to her almost identical companion, 'It's Benji!'

'No, no,' trills the other, hugging Lucky's neck, 'it's Greyfriars Bobby! Omigod, isn't he the hottest little thing!'

The girls are sartorial replicas of Paris Hilton; with them, on a bejewelled double-harness, are two miniature poodles, their snowy topknots caught in scarlet bows. The squealing 'toys' throw themselves at Lucky with even more zeal than their owners, licking and writhing like pop celebrities on Ecstasy. 'Koooork!' ('Let me at 'em!') snorts the sea dog with a gleam in his eye. But when he tries to mount one, the Paris lookalikes snatch up their tiny temptresses and clutch them to their chests.

'*Bad* Benji,' giggles Paris number one. She waves her poodle's paw at him. 'Jazzy says bye, bye beautiful Benji.'

Paris number two does the same: 'Snazzy says bye, bye beautiful Bobby.'

They flounce off. Lucky stares after them, then looks up at me as if to say, 'What the hell was *that* about?'

'Search me,' I tell him. 'I'm just the old dude on the other end of the rope.' (Neither Paris acknowledged or even looked at me during the encounter.)

Like most neutered dogs, Lucky's sexuality is an ongoing mystery. Until today, he's never responded to conventional 'targets', preferring surprise attacks on other males and compounding this perversity by sometimes tackling the biting end. His most ardent affair was with a green, corduroy-covered footstool he appropriated as his full-time lover, riding it about the lounge room to the delight of coarser guests. (Eventually, 'Ms Green' came apart at the seams and had to be retired.)

But that night, when we set off for the café, Lucky seems unusually keen to get back to the action in Hastings Street. He sniffs avidly around the seat where the poodles accosted him, and has to be half-dragged the rest of the way to the restaurant. We've been there about 30 minutes, with Lucky unusually quiet under the table, when a familiar cry cuts through the buzz of conversation. 'Omigod! Omigod! No! Stop it!'

Paris one and two rise abruptly from a table on the other side of the forecourt. There is the sound of something smashing, then more 'omigods!' followed by a clatter of falling chairs and a burst of wild laughter from a group of young men near the scene. As one, Scotty and I duck our heads to check on Lucky. Of course, the little bastard isn't there — just his leash and still-fastened collar.

By the time we reach the Paris table both girls are on their knees trying to get Lucky off the poodles. But Snazzy and Jazzy are so tangled in their dual leash they're effectively bound together, side by side, with Lucky astride both humping like he's never humped before.

'*Ménage à trios*! *Ménage à trios*!' hoots one of the young men. 'Go boy, go!'

'Shut up, arsehole!' hisses Paris one (or perhaps two), flailing at Lucky with her huge designer bag.

More plates crash from the table, which is being dragged around by the agitated poodles tethered to its leg. Being unencumbered, Lucky easily eludes the grasping hands and swinging bags, abandoning one position only to dart in from another angle and reclaim his prize.

Most diners near the action are now standing, glasses in hand, offering ribald commentary — 'Get a room! ... What a stud! ... Who's the main course?' — which seems to exhaust the Paris clones' reserves of cool.

'Get off, you little pig!' one of them yells.

'Hit him!' screeches the other. 'Hit him hard—'

'Lucky! No!' Scotty's voice cuts through the uproar, and he looks up, startled, as though snapped from a dream. Which is just enough of a distraction for me to pluck him off the poodles and wedge him under my arm.

The Paris girls endure our apologies without a word, or even a facial expression, though their eyes do widen when Lucky's paw starts waving at them.

'Lucky says bye, bye Snazzy and Jazzy,' I croon. 'Lucky says ...'

Scotty tows me back to our table.

FOURTEEN

Lucky takes almost a year to adjust to the absence of poor old Jake. For a while — apparently forgetting how he turned on his hero at the end — he reacts to any mention of Jake's name by jumping up excitedly and finding a high spot from which to cast around for him. When this proves futile, he scales back his response to rising briefly and then slumping down again with a cynical, older dog snort: 'Paaar!' ('He's *never* coming back!')

But the oddest effect of Jake's demise is the change in Lucky's attitude to Nick, who has finished his degree and moved back to Brisbane. In the early stages, whenever they meet, Lucky sets off on one of his exhaustive Jake hunts. Then he abandons this line of pathos and begins greeting Nick as though *he* is Jake. He's always liked Nick and his boisterous games, but suddenly this affection blossoms into the same yipping, leaping-for-joy love he once reserved for Jake alone.

In his mind, Nick and Jake have somehow morphed into the same entity. For a while, he even tries to hump Nick's leg — never a Lucky trait.

'Snap out of it!' I tell him. 'That's Nick, not Jake.'

'You're just jealous,' says Nick, prising Lucky from his ankle. 'That's why you invented this bizarre love-transference theory.' (But what would he know? Ascribing motives to animals is exacting work best left to experienced journalists.)

Soon after Jake's death, my daughter, Lou, returned from overseas and got a dog of her own. Finn (short for Finnigan) is a classic Jack Russell: good humoured, athletic and slightly mad. In short bursts, he and Lucky get on famously. But if they're together more than a few hours, Lucky's food mania kicks in and he claims all tucker in the house as his own. Despite this pattern and Lou's misgivings, I recklessly insist on looking after Finn for a week while she goes on holiday.

My plan is to feed the dogs separately, and for the first day it seems to be working. But on the second day, after scoffing his own meal in the front yard, Lucky somehow scales a high gate and drives Finn away from his meal in the backyard. After that, he launches a full-scale terror campaign, growling and snapping and applying the evil eye until Finn retreats to the spare room and won't come out.

He's bigger and stronger than Lucky, but nowhere near as crazy. And like those two shocked farm dogs years earlier, Finn isn't willing to test the outer limits of Lucky's volatility. We scold Lucky for his bullying, and even banish him temporarily to another room, but nothing will induce Finn to leave his place of exile.

On the third day of the stand-off, I phone Suzanne — the assistant at the veterinary clinic who cared for Lucky after he was abandoned — and explain the dilemma. She doesn't think food is the real problem.

'Lucky feels he owns you,' she says. 'He's not your dog, you're his people. You've given him the home he's obviously always wanted, and he's claimed you. He's gone, "These people are mine, and no other dog is getting them!"'

Later, watching Lucky in torpedo mode on the floor near my desk, I realise he's got one eye on me and the other on Finn, just visible inside the spare room. If I move, both eyes lock on me; if Finn moves, Lucky is on his feet in an instant, growling and moving to block his exit from the room. He doesn't sleep or change positions as he would normally, but maintains his vigil, hour after hour. Suzanne was right: it's not potential food sources he's keeping Finn away from, but me.

I stare into those steady brown eyes. 'You pushy little bastard,' I tell him.

'Kaark!' he says, and belly-crawls over to lick my hand.

Deep down, of course, I know damn well that Lucky's occasional tyranny stems from him being treated more like a family member than a conventional pet. But you can't have it both ways: over almost six years, the more we've grown to cherish Lucky the more lovable he has become. That was always the equation behind the 'friendly' approach, so as a friend we can hardly blame him when he pulls rank over visiting dogs.

Which is all very well ... but what will I tell Lou when she phones from the resort island to check on her beloved Finn?

The solution presents itself a bit later, when Lucky leaps up and rushes outside yipping joyously. It's Kelpie Man, my hybrid son, making a surprise visit. When he and Lucky have finished gambolling on the lawn, I explain the problem.

'Let me take Finn for the rest of the week,' he volunteers. 'It'll give us a chance to get acquainted.'

'Is that you offering, or Jake?'

'Same thing,' deadpans Nick. 'One body, one brain.' He produces his wallet, removes a headshot of Jake from the window (once occupied by a snap of his former girlfriend) and holds it next to his face. 'See?' He bares his teeth wolfishly. 'Identical. No wonder Lucky can't tell us apart.'

You do get weird about dogs. Over time, they become like a part of you that has learned to live externally. And when something bad happens (or almost happens) to them, anxiety over the incident can store itself inside you for a long time. Even now, thinking about Lucky teetering on the edge of Trady's deck on that wild night near Lady Musgrave Island fills me with dread. So does another awful moment, when a German shepherd sprang on him in a Bulimba park. From across the park, I watched horror-stricken as the snarling brute stood over Lucky with its fangs bared. Impeccably trained, the would-be killer responded instantly when its owner whistled it off with barely a pause in his power-walking.

A few nights ago, in a rare nightmare, another near-disaster returned to spring on me. For the most part, the dream mirrored what happened: a crowd of us leave a holiday house and walk to a nearby beach for a birthday party bonfire. We're drinking and singing, and Lucky (then with us less than a year) trots along among the forest of legs. But when we reach the bonfire, he's gone.

Scotty and I retrace our steps through soft sand cut by deep wheel tracks. Reaching the point where four-wheel-drive vehicles enter the beach from the road, we can see what happened: our footprints follow wheel tracks that swing left towards the bonfire; Lucky's prints, in another set of tracks, swing right — taking him in the opposite direction. It's a dark night, but our torch shows how Lucky plodded along in the same rut for hundreds of metres, even when it became so deep he couldn't see out. Then his prints disappear.

Some boys tell of seeing what they thought was a koala leave the beach and scamper up a hillside towards the local pub. We struggle up the slope, but there's no sign of Lucky. In front of the hotel is a busy main road, and there we find him: at the base of an embankment, right beside the stream of traffic. 'Lucky!' we yell, and he scrambles to our side. That's how it actually happened.

In the dream, though, there are no boys, no hillside, no pub. Just that sinister, ever-deepening wheel rut. We follow it interminably, even after it becomes so deep *we* can't see out. Lucky's prints are always visible, but there's some sort of trick involved: if we turn and head back the way we came, the prints lead that way too; turn again, and the prints reverse direction with us. Yet there is only one set of prints.

And that's it: we never find Lucky. It's one of those dreams you sense are dreams yet can't escape ... when I do wake, dry-mouthed, the elusive terrier is right there, draped across my pillow. Perhaps it was his snores that woke me, a type of symmetry often at play within the mysteries of sub-conscious/conscious circuitry.

Freudian analysts may disagree, but the dream itself seems pretty straightforward: disaster is always just one wrong turn away. Yet why all this retrospective angst over a dog, when the axiom applies equally to people?

Probably because of Lucky's vulnerability: ever since we got him, abandoned yet full of hope, I've had a minor phobia about keeping him safe. Actually, that's not quite right: the anxiety emerged over time, fed by memories of our own carelessness (as in the wheel-rut incident) early in the piece.

I can't bear the thought of Lucky ending up twice *un*lucky; of taking responsibility for him and then losing him, or somehow failing to live up to his trust. And though it makes little sense, I've finally realised what it is that makes him seem so vulnerable ... especially in my wheel-rut nightmare. It's his shortness: those improbable, bandy-arsed little legs. That's why he's always jumping and straining to see what's going on above ankle level.

Nothing makes him happier than a good vantage point or lookout: car headrests, the chart table, the top of Trady's cabin, verandas, people's necks, and so on. Only by climbing can the short-arsed terrier escape from the realm of dead bugs and skirting boards to a place more in keeping with his social standing.

FIFTEEN

Lucky's kamikaze cat attacks always seemed the greatest threat to his wellbeing, but in the end it's a lawn mower that lays him low. The saga begins on one of those hectic, pre-Christmas mornings when I try to squeeze in a bit of overdue mowing among a list of other chores. As usual, I confine Lucky to the house so he can't attack the noisy old two-stroke and try to gnaw off its wheels. But while I'm struggling to start the thing — with him yelping and leaping about inside — there's a crash of crockery from the kitchen, followed by a squeal of pain.

When I open the door to investigate, Lucky tears past me on three legs and tries to gnaw off the mower's wheels. 'What's going on out there?' calls Scotty from the shower. The broken plates on the kitchen floor tell the tale: mad terrier seeking elevation tries to clamber onto kitchen bench to access open window, but dislodges plates and crashes back to floor, hurting right front leg.

There's no blood on the injured leg, but he's holding it straight out in front of him, slightly raised, like some grotesque canine version of a Nazi salute. Yet it doesn't seem to be broken, and there are no more sounds of pain, so we assume it's either bruised or sprained. If he's still favouring it tomorrow, we'll take him to the vet for X-rays.

Giving up on the mower, we load Lucky into the car and set off to a nearby slipway for our next job: to collect *Tradewind*, just refloated after another round of improvements, and return her to the local marina. But by the time we get on board, with a two-hour trip ahead, we're starting to question our judgement about the seriousness of Lucky's injured leg. He still hasn't touched ground with it, and for the first time we can remember he allows the diesel to start without raging at the exhaust outlet.

As we wind down a shallow tidal river towards Moreton Bay, he stays curled beside me on the helmsman's seat, looking plaintive and slightly guilty. His incapacity changes the mood aboard; without an active short-arsed terrier, messing about on boats just doesn't seem the same. The ominous feeling builds when we clear the river and behold, in an otherwise clear sky, a black storm cell hovering above our marina. Instead of moving past it seems to wait for us, unleashing its real force just as we begin the tricky process of docking in the congested harbour.

Amid the drama, Lucky escapes into the driving rain and tears about the deck presenting his Nazi salute to the world. Battling to hold the tri in place while Scotty secures the shore lines, I can only watch as he falls on a turn and tumbles across the deck, almost going down between the boat and the dock. 'Stay!' I bellow over the wind. He crouches, wide-eyed and bedraggled, holding the injured limb off the deck. By the time Scotty gets to him and tucks him under her coat, we both know it's worse than a bruise or a sprain.

The X-rays confirm it: Lucky's fall has torn a ligament in his 'wrist' right off the bone. It's a serious injury, more complicated than a straightforward break, with the potential to leave him permanently crippled. As the vet explains this, Lucky — with a splint from shoulder to toe — is still sprawled in a recovery cage emerging from a knockout drug administered hours earlier. It'll be a month before the splint comes off and we know his long-term prospects; in the meantime, he's virtually confined to the house: no running, no boating or swimming, not even a sedate morning walk.

While the vet talks on, the sights and smells of the clinic draw me back to that day in Cooroy when Lucky came clickclickclicking into our lives. Can it really be only six years ago? He was about 18 months old then, and will soon enter his eighth year — in human terms, that'll make him 56: the same age as me. Yet I feel as though I've known him forever. More than that, he's the first dog whose future has always seemed inextricably bound with my own.

And now, if his injury is permanent ... what then? The deck of a sailboat is an unforgiving place for the physically impaired; even people with hip replacements have had to give up cruising after losing that innate sense of balance that can, in rough conditions, mean the difference between life and death. Would we go cruising without him? No way, I tell myself, knowing Scotty's response will be the same. The only alternative would be to abandon the Cruising Dream and see out Lucky's days in suburbia. I push these thoughts from my mind ... for the time being.

Lucky takes a long time to wake up; even when the vet's assistant emerges and places him in my arms he remains, apart from a moment of tail-wagging recognition, limp and groggy. At home, he sleeps all afternoon on a sofa with the splinted leg stuck out before him like a club. (Rock solid, the splint is formed by a U-shaped plastic frame that fits under the paw and up each side of the leg, bound in place by layers of heavy surgical tape.)

He stirs just before sunset, but when I look into his eyes there's no trace of awareness. He's conscious, but still 'missing', and when I carry him outside for a pee he just stands there with the splint raised, wobbling pathetically. Then he barks at me — two high, panicky notes ('Help!') — so I scoop him up and return him to the sofa.

He's still in limbo land when Scotty gets home from work; by 10 pm, we start to worry he may never emerge from his dose of 'Twilight', described by the vet as a blend of synthetic narcotic and a sedative/hypnotic akin to Rohypnol, the so-called date rape drug, with ten times the potency of Valium. Its effects are said to last from 4 to 12 hours ... yet at bedtime (more than 14 hours after his dose), Lucky's eyes remain as blank as beads.

Was he given too much? Suppressing our fears, all we can do is hope for the best. As usual, I'm the first to wake ... or the first human, because when I open my eyes just after sunrise Lucky is standing on the bed watching me.

'Kaark!' he says, and straight away I can see that the light has returned to those big brown eyes.

'He's back!' I cry.

After a hearty breakfast, the patient clunkclunkclunks about the wooden floors testing his makeshift new leg (and searching its tip for his seemingly missing paw), before heading outside to work on a technique for handicapped piddling.

And so it goes, week after week. As the vet warned, Lucky soon adjusts to the splint and thinks its protection makes him bulletproof. But whenever he exerts himself — a sudden bolt outside to investigate cat noises, or sometimes just hopping down from a sofa — pain follows. Then he hobbles about with the splint raised, or gives a disgusted snort — 'Kaar!' — and throws himself down in some darkened corner to brood.

Anti-inflammatory drops help ease his discomfort, but if used too often they can make him impervious to pain caused by over-exertion. That would expose him to the greatest danger of the healing period: pressure sores inside the splint, leading to gangrene and amputation — the fate of roughly half the dogs treated for such injuries. (According to the vet, who inspects Lucky's splint each week, active young dogs and explosive little terrier types are most at risk from pressure sores.)

But how, short of locking him in a cage, do you stop a terrier from tearing about? Especially one already depressed by the absence of morning walks, contact with his dog mates and ball games in the backyard, and who — despite the growing heat of summer — can't swim, or even take a proper bath.

During the worst period, when we keep the house shut to constrain him, Lucky grows so dejected he won't play, or 'buzz', or even growl from the window at the neighbour's cat.

'Cheer up, little boy,' cajoles Scotty. 'Just a couple more weeks, then you can be a mad bastard again. I promise!'

'Pwwwifff!' ('I'm so bored!') Lucky says. He gets up, clunks a few steps and slumps down again. He spends hours in torpedo mode staring at walls, and even gives up his beloved morning rough-house sessions on our bed. Eventually, in his misery and frustration, he starts chewing at the tape binding the splint to his shoulder.

'No!' one of us invariably calls, and he rises absolutely dejected and clunks off to another room. When he starts hiding from us to avoid these reprimands, we realise his confinement has become counterproductive. It's time for a distraction, and with good weather forecast — and a week till splint-removal day — we load Trady and head across the bay to spend a few days off Moreton Island.

Lucky is transformed. Sitting on deck with Scotty, he raises his snout to the sky and barks for the sheer hell of it. 'Wowowowo!' he rejoices, startling some hovering gulls. 'Wowowowo!' He hobbles to the end of his tether and grins up at me. 'Kaaark!' he snorts, over and over. ('This is more like it! Now you're talking! You beauty!')

We anchor off a secluded bay well south of the resort to avoid the holiday crowds and minimise encounters with our old foes the rangers. Lucky will have to go ashore twice a day, but getting sand or water in his splint at this stage could be a disaster, so we devise a waterproofing system before the first beach trip. (Two layers of heavy plastic bag over the splint, sealed at the shoulder with gaffer tape, and — the *pièce de résistance* — a rubber stubby cooler that fits snugly over the lower leg to stop shells ripping the plastic bags.)

It works a treat. Lucky has to stay on the leash to prevent him running or jumping in the water, but seems quite happy just clumping along the sand in his 'Mal's Baitshop' stubby cooler. Within a day, we all slip back into the rhythm of life aboard: Lucky patrolling the decks and fighting off seagull raids on his food; me and Scotty reading, napping, admiring our flash new electric toilet (no more pumping!), and luxuriating in the improved airflow from Trady's new cabin windows.

The only sour note comes on New Year's Eve, when the bay fills with drunken power-boaters. Always the least considerate neighbours, the 'stink-boat' set have a herd mentality and love to anchor right next to any vessel there when they arrive. By 8 pm, the yahoos are all around us, generators revving, TVs and stereos blaring and blinding flashlights arcing in all directions. Then four of the boats get even closer by 'rafting-up' (one boat remains anchored, while the others tie up on either side), and the party gets really wild.

We consider moving, but it is New Year's Eve — and drunks on boats can be entertaining — so we relax on deck to watch the show. It's amusing enough for a while: yahoos tumbling down stairs; yahoos falling overboard; yahoos trapping limbs between boats; yahoos wrapping themselves in Australian flags and shouting 'Oi, oi, oi!'; yahoos fighting, chundering, mooning the moon, and so on.

Just after midnight, as we toast Lucky's recovery and the long-awaited Year of the Cruising Dream, the yahoos start blasting emergency flares into the sky. They have no idea where the still-burning missiles will land, but there's every chance some will fall among the tinder-dry undergrowth of Moreton Island. (Destructive bushfires during previous summer seasons are thought to have been ignited in this way.)

'Hey fellas,' I call to the nearest boat when the flares keep flying. 'Watch out you don't cause a fire on the island.' That's all I say, yet the yahoos are instantly enraged. A dozen of them crowd to the boat's rail, bellowing abuse.

'Wowowowo!' responds Lucky from the cabin top.

'Shoot the dog! Shoot the fuckin dog!' shrieks a spotty flag wearer. And that's it:

red-mist time. I grab Lucky and put him in the cabin, and am on my way back with the spear gun when Leisa blocks the doorway.

'Don't be insane,' she pleads. 'They're dangerous morons. Take that gun outside, and anything could happen.' She's absolutely right.

I slump on the sofa, and the red mist slowly clears. 'Sorry,' I mutter, breathing deeply. 'It's all these new-look patriots. I didn't realise how much I hated them.'

Outside, the abuse is tailing off … apart from a few chicken noises. Then we hear a slurred voice: 'Look! The pricksar fugginorf. Yaa, fugorf then! Fugoorrrrf arseholes!'

Scotty and I exchange a look. Our 45-pound plough anchor has never dragged, even in winds over 40 knots, so it isn't us fugginorf. Which means — yes! — the rising tide has dislodged the poorly laid anchor of the rafted-up yahoos and is now bearing them southwards at about two knots. And they're so far gone they think it's us moving away from them!

'With a bit of luck,' says Scotty, checking the chart, 'they should tangle with that really big set of oyster banks about an hour from now. Hope they've got some flares left.'

New Year's morning 2007 is grey and unseasonably chilly as we ready the boat for the trip home. We've done it so often it's almost second nature: close and secure port vents, turn off gas at cylinders, ready sails, open saltwater intake valve and check oil and coolant levels before starting diesel and raising anchor. But even as the motor bursts to life I realise I've forgotten a new and vital stage: shut cabin door *before* starting diesel, to contain injured dog.

No, it's worse than that. I remember Lucky but simultaneously tell myself, 'Oh, he'll be okay', and turn the key. In the next awful, drawn-out moment I hear yelps of pain and rush on deck to find that Lucky, after jumping down to bark at the exhaust outlet, has jammed his splint between the wooden slats of the duckboard (or step), and is struggling frantically to free himself. I have to restrain his thrashing body with one arm while using the other to work the trapped leg free.

It takes only seconds, but when we get him into the cabin the splint is soaked and partially dislodged: in his desperation to be free of the trap Lucky has pulled the whole structure away from its shoulder bindings and dragged it 3–4 cm down his leg. We ease it back into position and wrap it in a towel to soak up the moisture, but there's no way of knowing what damage may have been done to the original injury. At least not until tomorrow, when the veterinary clinic re-opens after the holidays.

I can't think of a time when I've been so pissed off by my own stupidity. (Leisa isn't thrilled either, but maintains a diplomatic silence.) All those weeks of care and attention — not to mention Lucky's long-term mobility and the Cruising Dream itself — threatened by a single mindless moment. Too disgusted to bother with sails, I point Trady towards our distant marina and power grimly across the bay. Every so often another wave of recrimination strikes and I start muttering and raging like Captain Ahab … only crazier, and with no demonic whale to blame and curse, just myself.

It's the Lucky phobia thing again … the wheel-rut nightmare revisited … the cabin door carelessness repeated. But this time the intensity is unsettling: I know I'm being irrational, that mistakes happen, that a dog can't be made immune from danger. Yet I still feel guilt stricken. Why? It's not until that night, when I'm back at home watching the news, that an explanation (of sorts) presents itself.

I grab a pad. 'Have become victim of inter-cranial terrierism, a brain-hijacking fever induced by prolonged study of a small dog,' I write. 'In conventional form, terrierism strikes only hearts, infusing them with warm, irrational feelings called love. The virulent strain occurs when victim tries to write book about terrier, forcing brain to make sense of what heart is experiencing. As the two incompatible organs struggle to communicate, terrierism launches itself — synapsing wildly — from heart to brain, takes over and makes human assume responsibility for all the dog's woes.'

'You little bastard,' I tell Lucky, stirring his prone form with my foot. 'You've given me inter-cranial terrierism!'

He opens an eye. 'Prrwoik!' he snorts ('Piss off!'), and goes back to sleep.

Next morning, when he learns of the Duckboard Incident, the vet removes the splint a few days early rather than risk pressure sores. I hold Lucky still on the examination table as he works, and when the long-hidden 'wrist' joint emerges — still tender but healing well and apparently undamaged by yesterday's madness — it's a huge relief.

Lucky stares at his resurrected limb in apparent astonishment. 'Kaark!' he snorts, looking up at me as if to say, 'It was there all the time!'

He gives his paw a tentative nibble, then sets about it with a vengeance, working his teeth between the claws and going after all those long-unreachable itches. The leg muscles have shrunk from inactivity, and when we set him down Lucky still lifts the paw on every other step. But the vet says that's normal, and a few weeks of exercise should improve things.

'But nothing too strenuous,' he adds. 'The connective tissues are still adjusting, and if they get torn at this stage he could be laid-up for a long time.'

SIXTEEN

On a warm March night in 2007, some friends join us for dinner on board Trady. Nothing formal, just a pile of prawns and salad eaten as we stand about on deck in our berth at the marina. This is our friends' first time aboard and we enjoy their enthusiasm over the tri's home comforts and our cruising plans, now just *two months* away. They're impressed, too, by Lucky's on-board style.

'He's just so independent,' marvels one. 'I thought fluffy little dogs hung around all the time, like kids. But look …' — he points to the shadowy form on guard at the bow — '… he doesn't give a stuff about the rest of us. He's doing his own thing.'

'Doin' what he wants,' says Scotty, nudging me.

A couple of hours and bottles pass before I give Lucky another thought. We're all in the cabin by then, and he isn't visible from the windows, so I duck outside for a look around. The breeze has died leaving the water glassy calm, its dark surface glittering with reflected light. Lucky is lying by the edge of the deck intent on these dancing images. His head makes minute adjustments, and his ears fold and unfold to all the tiny sounds of the night.

'Hey, little mate.'

He looks up, eyes shining. 'Kaark!' he says as I ruffle his ears. But when I turn to leave, he jumps up and executes two quick circles — a recent addition to his communication range meaning, 'Don't go. Stay here.'

So I sit down beside him. 'Kaark!' he says again, resuming his position and pressing the side of his head into my palm.

And in that moment the real cause of my angst over Lucky's safety is finally revealed: I love him too much. If I didn't — and he was merely a conventional 'pet' — my responsibilities to him would be limited to food, exercise and shelter. But over seven years this remarkable, warm-hearted little critter has become one of us. So how can his wellbeing and happiness be less important than Scotty's, or mine, or that of others we hold dear? How bad would I feel if I caused Scotty to get lost in a dirty great wheel rut, or trap her splint in a duckboard?

Without realising it, I've allowed a lifetime of conditioning about what we can and can't feel about pets to cloud the truth ... which is that a small fluffy mongrel has stolen my heart. As we sit together on deck, I move my hand to Lucky's injured leg and wiggle the joint. No reaction. I apply more pressure (much more than he would have allowed a few weeks ago), yet all he does is lick my hand.

His post-splint improvement was frustratingly slow. For the first few weeks he limped a lot, and would lift the paw after just a few minutes of mild exercise. More troubling, he held his foot at an odd, twisted angle, as though it had set in the wrong position. But gradually, as the blend of fibrous and elastic tissue around the joint grew more supportive, everything came right. About a week after the last traces of limp disappeared, we were crossing a park on our morning walk with Lucky sniffing about far behind.

'Come on, slow coach!' called Scotty, and he began to run towards us.

'Yaa, go Lucky!' we yelled, spurring him on — a game he'd always loved before the injury. Ears in chaos, he ran faster and faster until his legs were a blur, flying past us with a triumphant grin before rounding up dramatically and waiting for us to catch up with him. That was the end of our doubts: the sea dog was back on deck, and the Cruising Dream was coming true at last.

And now, watching the dance of the marina lights, I wonder if Lucky's new, two-circles message ('Don't go! Stay here!') means he's entering a calmer, more reflective stage. Perhaps his recent trials have diffused his madder impulses, made him more appreciative of life's quieter moments. Then he sees something — a tiny flicker in the water next to the hull, and jumps to his feet.

'Grrrr!'

He glares down from the edge of the deck. It's a ... PUFFER FISH! Here, touching *his* boat!

'GRRRRRR!'

He rears up and down on the spot like a tiny, enraged bison, pounding the deck with his feet, then rips twice around the boat before springing to the top of the cabin and lifting his outraged face to the moon.

'Wowowowo!' he thunders, as though petitioning the gods for justice. 'Wowowowo!'

Listen out for him. He's still quite mad, and he could be coming to a port near you.

FRANK ROBSON was born in New Zealand, and spent an itinerate, jack-of-all-trades existence in Australia before becoming a journalist. He has worked for numerous publications, from the Melbourne *Truth* to *Time*, run a freelance press agency, made documentaries, and written two previous books: *Dare to be Different* (on Queensland oddballs), and a novel, *Food of Fools*. Robson has won two Walkley Awards for feature writing, and until recently was a full-time writer with *Good Weekend* magazine.

126.